"Just what the doctor ordered! Filled with stories from April's life as well as her readers' lives, *The Peaceful Mom* brings wisdom and peace to the table during times of potential stress for any mom with kids in the house. Be prepared for many hard questions that will facilitate growth for you. This book is especially powerful for moms who struggle with living vicariously through their children's lives."

—NINA ROESNER, executive director of Greater Impact Ministries, and coauthor of *With All Due Respect*

"As moms, we often  ontrol and make everything turn out ' nly creates stress, anxiety, perfectionis :alming wisdom, April invites us to finu ᵥᵤₐₜ ᵥₙₑ ₗₑₑ ₑe that only comes from knowing Jesus and laying control before His throne. This book is rooted in God's Word and filled with practical help for finding balance as a responsible and peaceful mom."

—SHANNON POPKIN, author of *Control Girl*

PRAISE FOR *THE PEACEFUL WIFE*

"April knows what it's like to struggle in her marriage with frustration and anger toward her spouse. Her journey to becoming a peaceful wife will resonate with any reader who wants new peace in her own marriage. I love that this book walks each of us through the reality checks we need in order to have the marriage we want!"

—SHAUNTI FELDHAHN, social researcher, and best-selling author of *For Women Only*

"April Cassidy has written an excellent book! I endorse her heart and message. In fact, I asked my daughter-in-law to read it and she reported to me, 'April does an excellent job of placing a mirror in front of readers so that they may see the ways they have been disrespectful, but she also provides a comforting hug as she explains how the disrespect can end and a life of respecting one's husband can move into place. She provides great insight into her own struggles and a wonderful chapter where her own husband gives his thoughts on her transformation. April challenges, encourages, and breathes hope for all wives.'"

—EMERSON EGGERICHS, author of *Love and Respect*

APRIL CASSIDY

The Peaceful Mom

Building a healthy foundation with

Christ AS Lord

Kregel
Publications

The Peaceful Mom: Building a Healthy Foundation with Christ as Lord
© 2018 by April Cassidy

Published by Kregel Publications, a division of Kregel Inc., 2450 Oak Industrial Dr. NE, Grand Rapids, MI 49505.

The author and publisher are not engaged in rendering medical or psychological services, and this book is not intended as a guide to diagnose or treat medical or psychological problems. If medical, psychological, or other expert assistance is required, the reader should seek the services of a health-care provider or certified counselor.

Personal stories have been used by permission. In some cases, names and identifying details have been changed to protect the privacy of the individuals involved.

All Scripture quotations, unless otherwise indicated, are from the Holy Bible, New International Version®, NIV®. Copyright © 1973, 1978, 1984, 2011 by Biblica, Inc.™ Used by permission of Zondervan. All rights reserved worldwide. www.zondervan.com

Scripture quotations marked HCSB are from the Holman Christian Standard Bible®, Copyright © 1999, 2000, 2002, 2003, 2009 by Holman Bible Publishers. Used by permission. HCSB® is a federally registered trademark of Holman Bible Publishers.

ISBN 978-0-8254-4463-0

Printed in the United States of America
18 19 20 21 22 23 24 25 26 27 / 5 4 3 2 1

*I dedicate this book to my husband, Greg,
and our two children for their love and patience as I continue
to learn to become a more peaceful mom and wife. I pray that
God will make me a blessing to them.*

I'm very thankful for the support of The Peaceful Wife *blog
readers, for their feedback, support, love, prayers, and stories.
I also dedicate this book to them. What an honor to be on this
journey together as sisters in Christ!*

Contents

Introduction

Every mother I know wants to be a great mom. We want to model healthy ways of relating and living for our children in every area of our lives. We want to live in tranquility, harmony, and joy in our families. But sometimes our dreams for our families and ourselves don't match our everyday lives very well. Many of us beat ourselves up over our failures and struggle to find direction for the next step.

God has provided for those who belong to Christ to live in spiritual abundance, but many of us are missing out on His treasures. Thankfully, we don't have to live our lives in turmoil. God has provided a path for us, and if we follow it and receive all that the Lord has for us, we will be peaceful moms.

A peaceful mom knows God intimately and follows Him wholeheartedly. Her heart is increasingly filled to overflowing with the spiritual treasures of Christ.

A peaceful mom has peace with all the following:

God	Her circumstances
Her thoughts	Her future
Her heart	Death
Others	Her eternal destiny

Doesn't that sound lovely? God makes His peace available to anyone who wants to wholeheartedly love and know Him. My prayer is that we might each see how good God is and choose to respect His gracious terms. There are countless spiritual riches to be had when we truly grasp that Jesus is the greatest treasure there is.

> The kingdom of heaven is like treasure hidden in a field. When a man found it, he hid it again, and then in his joy went and sold all he had and bought that field. (Matt. 13:44)

> If only you had paid attention to my commands,
> your peace would have been like a river,
> your well-being like the waves of the sea. (Isa. 48:18)

THE PATH TO BECOMING A PEACEFUL MOM

In God's great wisdom, He created everything that exists. He had good purposes for every planet, star, plant, and animal—with the primary purpose being to bring glory to Himself.

> The heavens declare the glory of God;
> the skies proclaim the work of his hands.
> Day after day they pour forth speech;
> night after night they reveal knowledge. (Ps. 19:1–2)

So regardless of life circumstances, the journey to becoming peaceful moms starts with our relationship with God, with His purpose for us. He tells us that we were created as individuals and as families to bring glory to our Creator. God gave people a unique position in creation. The other creatures and things He made have no choice. They cannot choose to rebel against Him or love Him. But God has given this powerful choice to each of us.

> This is what the LORD says:
> "Stand at the crossroads and look;
> ask for the ancient paths,
> ask where the good way is, and walk in it,
> and you will find rest for your souls." (Jer. 6:16)

What will we do with this incredible gift of choice? Will we seek God's will and exalt Him in our lives, or will we seek glory for ourselves and go our own way?

How we live out the answer to that question directly relates to how much peace we have in our lives. Jesus, who is God in the flesh, is the Prince of Peace (Isa. 9:6). To know Him intimately and to be one in spirit with Him is peace. There is no other source of genuine peace, tranquility, and spiritual rest for anyone. In a world where fears constantly bombard us and few people experience genuine peace, we have the opportunity to take a better path. When we take that path, we can introduce our children to that way as well. It's a "narrow" and unpopular path that not many find, but God has made it readily available to each of us.

> Enter through the narrow gate. For wide is the gate and broad
> is the road that leads to destruction, and many enter through
> it. But small is the gate and narrow the road that leads to life,
> and only a few find it. (Matt. 7:13–14)

> Jesus answered, "I am the way and the truth and the life. No
> one comes to the Father except through me." (John 14:6)

I never really experienced peace until 2009. For all my life up until that point, my head was always spinning with worry and fear. I spent every waking moment trying to figure out how I was going to make everything turn out right. I felt so much pressure, believing that everything depended totally on me.

When I began to truly yield to Christ as Lord for the first time and to trust Him, I was not prepared for what would happen. One day I realized that my mind was not spinning like crazy. The tightness was gone from my chest. I felt like I could breathe. My heart felt light. My mind was clear and free. I was not worried or stressed.

> There is only one source of genuine
> peace: the Lord Jesus Christ.

At first, I was confused. *What is all this open space in my mind and heart?* I wondered. And then it hit me. *Oh! This is peace! Wow. What a beautiful thing! I want to live like this for the rest of my life!* Now my prayer is that you will also experience this most addictive, supernatural gift from God as you get to know Him yourself.

Thankfully, any of us can be a peaceful mom. That is such great news to many exhausted, stressed-out, worried moms everywhere!

OVERFLOWING PEACE

As we allow God to transform us, not only do we benefit, but His peace also begins to permeate our homes and families. After we've looked at how to grow in our relationship with God, we'll explore how His goodness spills out into our relationships with others, blessing them too and gently calling them to find His peace and rest for their souls.

I invite you to join me on the adventure of a lifetime. Let's look together at the little baby steps we can take to move from fear, worry, anxiety, and exhaustion to peace, joy, and fulfillment, which are available to us in Jesus.

This book is meant to be digested slowly. Take your time. Allow God to speak to your heart. Be willing to dig as deeply as necessary. You may even want to reread portions over again later to really let God's truth and power sink in. I'd love for us to walk this road together. That is the beauty of being part of the body of Christ. We don't have to do this alone!

A PEACEFUL MOM'S PRAYER

Lord,

Thank You that You alone are God and there is no other. Thank You for Jesus and for the cross and the life You have provided for us if we will receive it. Thank You for marriage, family, and children. We praise You for Your love for us. Thank You for Your good design for families and for strong, loving relationships. Thank You that You have incredible wisdom to share with each of us. Help us to slow down and rest at Your feet so that we might absorb the blessings You have for us in Your Word and in relationship with You. Please give us ears that are sensitive to Your voice, which speaks to us softly today. We thank You for Your promise to those who belong to You: "Whether you turn to the right or to the left, your ears will hear a voice behind you, saying, 'This is the way; walk in it'" (Isa. 30:21).

In the name and power of Christ, amen.

Part One

God and Me

Examining the Throne of My Heart

Jesus answered, "It is written: 'Worship the Lord your
God and serve him only.'" (Luke 4:8)

Many people grew up in churches believing that if they only prayed a few sentences of a prayer after a pastor at church or a rally that they were "saved." They thought if they just believed that Jesus died and was raised to life again and they said the words of a particular spoken prayer, they had their golden ticket to heaven!

Perhaps they believed there was nothing else involved in following Christ. Or maybe some thought that after they prayed that prayer, they needed to figure out how to be the perfect Christian in their own strength. If they just tried hard enough, they could be good enough in God's eyes.

> Now this is eternal life: that they know you, the only true God, and Jesus Christ, whom you have sent. (John 17:3)

I can remember thinking, as a child, that Jesus didn't do a very good job of explaining the gospel. I mean, He never talked about inviting

Him into my heart. He never talked about praying a certain kind of prayer to be saved or about coming forward during an invitation time after the church service.

He said things like this:

- "Come, follow me" (Matt. 4:19).
- "Whoever wants to be my disciple must deny themselves and take up their cross and follow me" (Matt. 16:24).
- "A new command I give you: Love one another. As I have loved you, so you must love one another. By this everyone will know that you are my disciples, if you love one another" (John 13:34–35).
- "Anyone who loves me will obey my teaching. My Father will love them, and we will come to them and make our home with them. Anyone who does not love me will not obey my teaching" (John 14:23–24).

It turns out that Jesus knew how to explain the gospel. I was the one who was confused. Jesus wants me to know Him deeply. He wants me to be one in Spirit with Him. He wants me to follow Him spiritually every day for the rest of my life. This is not a distant head-knowledge. It's not like, "I know who the president of the United States is, but I have never met him." This is a profoundly life-changing kind of "knowing" that He is talking about. The demons know about Jesus and tremble, but they do not belong to Him! Jesus invites me to be adopted into God's family, to become God's child. What an incredible offer!

If I want to truly know God and belong to Him as His daughter, there is radical commitment involved on my part. I must be willing to live with God on a daily basis and to invite Him into every area of my life. He is now my Father and Lord, so anything that is my business is now His business and I am now under His loving authority.

The first step in becoming a peaceful mom is to decide to give Jesus control of my life from now on. Peace comes when Jesus is Lord of absolutely every area of life. There is no genuine peace apart from me living in surrender to His lordship. (For more on how to become a Christian, please check out appendix A.)

> You will keep in perfect peace
>> those whose minds are steadfast,
>> because they trust in you. (Isa. 26:3)

> Jesus said, "If you hold to my teaching, you are really my disciples. Then you will know the truth, and the truth will set you free." (John 8:31–32)

A Committed Follower

Of course, surrendering all *sounds* easy, but putting it into practice is considerably more difficult. For many years, I thought I was a pretty amazing Christian woman, wife, and mom. I knew the Bible inside and out and read it daily. I could quote many verses from memory, and I prayed daily during my quiet time. Then I also prayed throughout the rest of the day. I only listened to Christian music. I said I trusted God, and I thought I really did trust God.

But there was a disconnect. The fruit of my life didn't match what I said I believed. I was perfectionistic and worried almost constantly. Fear and "what-ifs" fueled my thinking and motives. People pleasing seemed like a godly thing even though it left me empty, stressed, and lonely. I was impatient when my children took too long to do things and would often snap at them in frustration. Yet somehow, I didn't see that anything was wrong.

My mind-set included things like these:

- "Worry is love. If I'm not worried about someone, it must only mean that I don't love them."
- "I have to figure everything out. If I don't, this will all end in

disaster! I am the only one who can prevent total chaos from happening."

- "I need to try to control everything in my children's lives to try to protect them and keep them safe."
- "Of course I have a lot of fear. There are so many things to be afraid of. Have you seen the news today?"
- "I can't ever let anything bad happen to my kids, or I am a complete failure as a mom!"
- "Of course I trust God, *but* I have to make sure my kids turn out right. And I feel the pressure on my shoulders to get this done properly."
- "I am always right, and if someone disagrees with me, that person is wrong."
- "People need to do what I want them to do, and things will be great."
- "I need to take charge, or nothing will get done right."
- "Other people don't know God's will like I do. They need my wisdom and direction."

The whole time, I was reading God's Word and His promises and singing about trusting Him completely and surrendering all to Him. I was doing so many right things, but still somehow I had it all wrong. I had deceived myself about my deepest motives. There were a lot of areas where I did not really trust God. My faith was in myself more than God, and I was miserable because of it.

"The real test of my faith . . . is the fruit of my life."

The real test of my faith is not what I think or say I believe—but rather, it is the fruit of my life. If I am living in the power of God, His Spirit will so fill me and radically transform me to be more and more like Him that I will exhibit the fruit of the Holy Spirit on a daily basis. It will be noticeable to everyone around me.

I will love all people with the very love of God. I will think with His mind, love with His heart, and see with His eyes. I will respond with His character. He will literally live through me because He will be in control, not me.

> But the fruit of the Spirit is love, joy, peace, forbearance, kindness, goodness, faithfulness, gentleness and self-control. (Gal. 5:22–23)

> Love is patient, love is kind. It does not envy, it does not boast, it is not proud. It does not dishonor others, it is not self-seeking, it is not easily angered, it keeps no record of wrongs. Love does not delight in evil but rejoices with the truth. It always protects, always trusts, always hopes, always perseveres. Love never fails. (1 Cor. 13:4–8)

This is not about me trying really hard or about total sinless perfection. It is not about any goodness in myself. It is about me resting in the work and power of Christ and allowing Him to have full control as Lord of *all* in my life. He is worthy to sit on the throne of my heart with nothing else above or beside Him. I have to guard my heart about this because it is so easy to let something slip ahead of Him in my priorities and not even realize it.

OUR DESTRUCTIVE IDOLS

I find it helpful to do a "throne check" often. I might pray, "Lord, are each of these things from Galatians 5:22–23 and 1 Corinthians 13:4–8 true in my life right now? Show me where I am missing the mark so I can turn away from anything that displeases You. I want to hate what You hate and love what You love. I want to tear out every wrong way of thinking and make any changes You want me to make. I am fully Yours!"

I need to ask God to help me examine myself, inviting Him to shine His holy light on the deepest, most hidden places in my heart and mind. Then I can accurately see my true motives and recognize any lies I may have embraced or wrong fixed beliefs upon which I may have built my faith or my life.

> Search me, God, and know my heart;
>   test me and know my anxious thoughts.
>   See if there is any offensive way in me,
>   and lead me in the way everlasting. (Ps. 139:23–24)

These "throne checks" are especially important when I find myself lacking peace and feeling overwhelmed, afraid, worried, angry, disappointed, or upset. These negative emotions are a gift from God. I like to think of them as an alarm that something may be wrong—similar to an indicator light flashing a warning on my car's dashboard.

Sometimes negative feelings are simply a signal that I am exhausted, hungry, hormonal, or sick. If there is a physical need my body has, I want to try to take care of that need first, and then I will be able to more accurately assess if there are other problems going on spiritually as well.

Beyond physical needs, my negative feelings might indicate that someone is sinning against me or someone else. If that is the case, I may have righteous anger against sin that I need to deal with in a constructive way (which we will discuss later in chapter 4).

Negative feelings could be a signal that there has been a misunderstanding or simply differing expectations that need to be addressed in a relationship. Perhaps I need to humbly speak with the person with whom I am upset and ask some gentle questions to better understand that person's perspective. When I can understand someone else's thought processes, I may find that I don't have negative feelings anymore.

But there are also times that negative feelings are a sign that I am cherishing sin in my heart. If I allow something in my life to take precedence over God, it becomes a sin. At that point, I've broken my spiritual intimacy and fellowship with God—not my relationship with Him, but our spiritual and emotional connection. Our "fellowship." He has healthy boundaries with me. He can't let me be close to Him when I am covered in something nasty and repulsive to His holiness. This results in me feeling pain because I miss His goodness, His peace, and His presence. That pain should gently remind me to trash the sinful thing in my life and humbly run back to Jesus in my heart and mind.

> ## "Negative feelings often let me know I need to examine my heart."

Those negative feelings often let me know I need to examine my heart. I can check my heart's throne by prayerfully asking some probing questions about my motives and priorities during my prayer time with God:

- What are my greatest fears?
- Why am I feeling so upset right now? What is the root issue?
- What do I believe I need in order to be content?
- What are my most precious dreams?
- What do I complain about the most?
- Can I be content if I do not get what I want?
- If I am feeling disappointed, is it possible that I am trusting a person or thing more than I am trusting God?
- If I am feeling worried, is there some area where I believe God could "get it wrong"?
- On what things (other than God) do I depend for my contentment, fulfillment, and security?
- In what areas do I take pride in a sinful way?

- How am I seeking self, self-will, or self-exaltation?
- How am I humbly seeking God, His will, and His glory alone?
- What things, people, or circumstances do I refuse to give up for whatever He wants?
- How can I work toward releasing those things I may be holding back from God?
- Do my thoughts, words, tone of voice, body language, and actions match what I say I believe about God?
- How am I doing at freely laying down everything and everyone in my life before God? Am I trusting Him completely with all of it, not knowing what the future may hold?

When I ask myself these kinds of questions and invite God's Spirit to search my heart, He can illuminate my hidden motives. My greatest fears often are that I will lose my idols. Fear and idolatry work hand in hand. Idolatry happens when I desire something or someone more than I desire Jesus. Because I don't have my trust in something that is unshakable, and I know I may not receive or keep the things I desire so strongly, I have great fear. I don't trust God and His wisdom to know what is best. Whenever I notice big fear, it is a good idea for me to ask God to help me evaluate if I may have a related desire as an idol in my heart.

An idol is often something I think I can't live without.

The Greatest Commandment, according to Jesus, is to "Love the Lord your God with all your heart and with all your soul and with all your mind" (Matt. 22:37). If I love something or someone else with all my heart, soul, and mind, I am putting that other thing or person in God's rightful place in my life. The thing I want may be good. It may even be a gift from God. But if I want it more than I want Jesus, I am dealing with an idol. An idol is anything I look to for my greatest sense of peace, security, hope, identity, contentment, and happiness. I can make anything or anyone in my life into an idol.

Idols always destroy me, robbing me of peace. They are worthless to help or save me. They don't have God's power. They are not God. They cannot meet the deepest needs of my heart. Idolatry has been the downfall of God's people throughout history. An idol is an addiction. It is something—even something good—that I love so much more than anything else, I am willing to do anything to have it. I might be willing to sin to get it. I may even desperately think, "I can't live without this! I *have* to have it!"

These are some of the common idols in our culture:

Self	Children
Happiness	Money
Being right	Luxury
Love	Fame
Romance	The American dream
Youth	Power
Beauty	Security
Pleasure	Worldly success
Having control	Health
Marriage	Education
Husband/Wife	Career
Parents	Politics

What I may not realize is that when self or anything/anyone else is on the throne of my life, I am actually living as an enemy of God. Idols are all about self and doing things my way rather than God's way. They are about putting my faith in things other than the Lord. The paycheck that I earn from living for self is pretty horrific. According to the Bible, my wage for this approach is separation from God (Rom.

6:23). Trusting self is the path to being an anxious, fearful, lonely, angry mom . . . far from being a peaceful mom. When I am living in the power of self, the results are predictably bad in this life and (if I don't know Christ) in the next—eternal separation from God and from everything that is good.

> The acts of the flesh are obvious: sexual immorality, impurity and debauchery; idolatry and witchcraft; hatred, discord, jealousy, fits of rage, selfish ambition, dissensions, factions and envy; drunkenness, orgies, and the like. I warn you, as I did before, that those who live like this will not inherit the kingdom of God. (Gal. 5:19–21)

> The one who does what is right is righteous, just as he is righteous. The one who does what is sinful is of the devil, because the devil has been sinning from the beginning. The reason the Son of God appeared was to destroy the devil's work. No one who is born of God will continue to sin [as a habit], because God's seed remains in them; they cannot go on sinning, because they have been born of God. (1 John 3:7–9)

Grateful Submission

When I yield the throne of my life to the lordship of Christ, I can live in thankfulness, peace with God, and joy. I no longer am a slave to sin. Now I have been set free to live a new kind of life for God!

> I have been crucified with Christ and I no longer live, but Christ lives in me. The life I now live in the body, I live by faith in the Son of God, who loved me and gave himself for me. (Gal. 2:20)

> Therefore, if anyone is in Christ, the new creation has come: The old has gone, the new is here! (2 Cor. 5:17)

When I read about confessing Him as Savior and Lord, it is easy to gloss over the word *Lord* without much thought about the staggering implications of making Christ the Lord of my life. This will dramatically impact every motive of my heart, every thought in my mind, and every decision I make.

If I choose to follow Jesus as Lord, God will change my heart so that I will hate sin like He does. God gives me a new Spirit, His Spirit, that changes my heart and desires to match His own. I will want to do God's will. I will have a spiritual appetite for God's presence, His will, and His Word. I will want to hear God's voice of correction and ask God to show me my blind spots, even if it is painful. I will want to follow and obey Him. I will want to grow in Him. The moment I see sin in my life, I will beg God to help me get rid of it and be restored back to right fellowship with Him. If I profess Christ but am content to live in habitual sin, something is terribly wrong.

> "When Jesus is my Lord, I am willing to bend to His will no matter what the cost may be."

When Jesus is my Lord, I am willing to bend to His will no matter what the cost may be to me. I may have to wrestle at times to get to that point, but this will be my goal. He is the only one worthy of this level of sacrifice. I give all of myself for Him. Not begrudgingly or with any resentment, but I surrender myself with overflowing joy and gratitude because I realize the depth of the price He paid for my sins on the cross. How can I do anything but want to please Him now?

Jesus has given me all of His goodness and right standing with God. He has given me constant and immediate access to the Holy of Holies that even the high priests didn't have in Israel before Christ came. No mere human had this kind of access to God before Jesus made it all available to believers through the cross. What a priceless gift!

He has provided thousands of promises in Scripture that no one can steal from me. He took away my hopelessness and helplessness and replaced it with His overwhelming holiness and power to obey God. Jesus's lordship in my life is not a burden but the most divine gift and calling there is!

I lay down these aspects of my life:

Career	Past
Trust	Health
Will	Money
Wisdom	Greatest fears
Marriage	Priorities
Children	Desires
Most precious dreams	Energy
Emotions	Fixed beliefs
Future	Possessions

I have no way to have peace with God in my own power. I have no ability to impress God. I owe a massive debt to God that I cannot pay. I deserve God's condemnation and separation from God in hell, according to the Bible. What incredible love God has for me that Jesus made it possible for me to have peace with God if I will receive His gift of His death and resurrection for me. Peace with God is the greatest peace there is. It is the source from which all other peace flows. The first key to being a peaceful mom is to invite the Prince of Peace to rule my heart.

LETTING GO OF MY WILL —NANCY'S STORY

I discovered more than once that the Lord was *not* on the throne when I came to the point of despair of ever getting God's will right in my life. I could see His will. Or so I thought. I believed I would have to do specific things to see that will accomplished. I thought my will was what He wanted, but, it turns out, it wasn't at all. My will was in the way of His will every time.

After I spent so much time praying for His will to be done, but not seeing it get done, the Lord always brought me back to the cross, where I realized that I can do nothing. I can't bring about His will. I realized that if it was His will, if He wanted anything done or accomplished, *He* must do it in and through me! The only way that He would come in with His Spirit and power was if I yielded all personal self-interest to the cross.

I had to recognize and acknowledge that my desires for other things were really lord in my life at that time. I would have to let go of my will in order to give God His rightful place as Lord over every area of my life. Then I could see Him work out His own will and purposes in my life!

It always comes down to the cross and back to the starting place of "I can do nothing in myself!" I also must come to the place where I am sifted of all self-interests and I have an undivided heart for the Lord. When He alone has become the sole object of my desire, the way is opened for the Lord to come in with His Spirit and power to do what only He can do for His own purposes and glory. True peace and rest flood my heart when I yield all that is personal to the cross and become one with Him in His purpose of bringing Christ as Lord into every area of life.

Ironically, when I come to this place in spirit and in truth, I find that He works it all for my good. I gain a blessing in having let go of my will, my desires, and even what I mistakenly thought the Lord wanted. When He has truly come into His place as Lord in my heart, my marriage, my parenting, my job, etc. . . . . I find that my own heart is satisfied. There is joy, there is peace, and most importantly, the Lord is satisfied and I find His presence.

A Peaceful Mom's Prayer

Lord,

From this day on, I want to keep You squarely on the throne of my life. I know I have been tempted to put myself and other things or people in that place that only belongs rightfully to You. Help me to recognize when I begin to allow other things to creep in and push You out. Help me to consciously set You on the throne daily and to seek to exalt, obey, and honor You as Lord. I submit my whole life to You and all that I am. I am Yours, and You are my God! Take my life and do what You want to do with it. I trust You. I no longer trust myself.

Amen.

Putting My Oxygen Mask On First

*Come to me, all you who are weary and burdened, and I
will give you rest. (Matthew 11:28)*

An airline steward gives a preflight safety demonstration as passengers wait for the plane to take off. He explains that if the cabin air pressure drops in-flight, oxygen masks will fall from the ceiling above each passenger. Airlines instruct parents to put their own masks on first and then to put the masks on their children. If a mom tries to take care of her children first but loses consciousness before she can get her own mask on properly, she is not going to be able to help them or herself.

When my children were young, I tended to think that being a "good mom" meant I could never take care of myself. Of course, I am not to be selfish and ignore my children's legitimate needs. But there is balance required here, as in every other area of my walk with Christ. Is it really selfish for a mom to put some limits on her children at certain times so she can take care of her needs?

Why Mom Needs Oxygen First

Without proper rest, time, and brain space, it's quite impossible for a mom to be connected to God. And without that connection, the family quickly spins out of control. A mom has to be filled up and nourished physically and spiritually before she has the ability to meet the needs of her children. God didn't create any of us to be superwoman, even if that is the message we receive in our culture today. We need nourishment, soul rest, and physical rest. God made people, even mothers, with certain limitations. This forces us to acknowledge our dependence on Him and to admit that we truly can't "do it all."

In addition, God designed families with parents in charge. Scripture is clear that my children need their parents to be in charge. If they believe they are in control of everything, it is way too much weight on their shoulders. Kindergarchy—when children rule the home—is not God's design for families and for good reason. In fact, Proverbs 22:15 says, "Folly is bound up in the heart of a child." That is why children need wise, experienced, loving adults to be in charge. When we implement God's design for families, everyone in the home can better experience God's peace. If we invert His authority structure at any point, there will be chaos.

> "An appropriate no is just as much of a gift and blessing to my children as an appropriate yes."

I don't want to be so afraid to upset my children that I allow myself to be held hostage to my children's every whim and desire. I can be kind and loving. I can be gentle, respectful, and firm, when necessary. I do not have to say yes to everything my children want me to do. In fact, it is imperative that I learn when to say no to my children. An appropriate no is just as much of a gift and blessing to my children as an appropriate yes. Even if they don't like it at the time.

Finally, if it's my job to raise godly children who live peaceful lives, I would suggest that it is a blessing to my family (and the world around us) when I teach my children that Mom and all other people have legitimate needs, too. I don't want to put my needs ahead of my children in a selfish way and make our family "all about me all the time." But my children do need to know that I am a real person who has limitations. As they grow older, they also need to learn to respect that other people have needs and that the entire world does not revolve completely around them. This helps them develop compassion, empathy, and understanding for the needs of other people.

WHEN I NEED TO PUT MY NEEDS FIRST AS A MOM

There are times when it is appropriate and necessary for me to put my needs ahead of my children's, particularly if the children don't have any urgent needs at the moment.

> Do nothing out of selfish ambition or vain conceit. Rather, in humility value others above yourselves, not looking to your own interests but each of you to the interests of the others. (Phil. 2:3–4)

It is easy sometimes for us as women to read this verse to mean we can only look out for other people's needs. But notice that we are supposed to look to our needs as well. The key, as with almost everything in the Christian life, is healthy balance.

If a mother is so busy feeding her children that she doesn't eat at all and she continues doing this long enough, she will eventually not be able to function. If a mom allows her children to interrupt her sleep for years even when the children are not ill and not in need, she will be so sleep deprived that she will not be able to give her best to God, her husband, her children, or anyone else.

There are times we need to put our children's needs first, absolutely. If an infant is going through a growth spurt at two weeks of age and needs to be nursed every hour or so for a few days, a loving mom will care for her baby's need. Or if a child is sick in the night, a good mom will set aside her own legitimate need for sleep to take care of the emergency.

But what about times when it is more about habits rather than emergencies and true needs? What if a toddler is still getting up multiple times in the night to come nurse or hug Mom and is not sick or hurt and everything is fine? Is it a gift to the family for the mom to continue to allow this habit to go on indefinitely when it jeopardizes her own health, sanity, and ability to be the wife and mom God calls her to be?

"It's important to think about the big picture, not just the next five minutes."

It's my responsibility as a mother to consider God's Word, my own needs, my husband's needs, and our children's needs. I am to use godly discernment and wisdom as I make decisions that are best for everyone involved. It's important to think about the big picture, not just the next five minutes.

Here are some questions I might ask myself when I am not sure whose needs should be the priority:

- What will be the greater gift to my children, my husband, my marriage, and each person's health (spiritually, emotionally, and physically) in the long run?
- Which course of action will most honor God?
- What are the consequences to our marriage and to our family if I continue to allow this to happen when there is not truly an emergency?
- What does my husband (or a godly mentoring wife/mom, if I don't have a husband) think might be a viable solution to the problem? Could God be leading me through him and his insights?
- What do I need to do to be sure I can think clearly at the moment and hear God's wisdom and discernment?

- Am I responding out of guilt, fear, anger, bitterness, exhaustion, or genuine love?
- Is this how I hope my children will act when they have their own families?

But there are times when it is absolutely necessary for me to put my needs first.

When I Have a Medical Emergency

If my blood sugar is dropping dangerously low and I realize I am going to pass out soon, I need to let my husband and children (or whoever is there or could come to help me) know that I need help. Or I need to do everything I can to get help for myself before I become incapacitated. I may need to quickly try to get the car into a parking lot if I am driving.

If I am extremely sick or wounded, I need to call for an ambulance or ask someone to get me to the hospital rather than trying to take care of fixing supper or doing chores. If I am pregnant and begin to bleed in my first or second trimester, I need to ask for help so I can lie down and stay on bed rest and call the doctor.

Yes, it is good to take care of others and be selfless, but if I am having a true emergency, I need to take care of my health so I can be around to continue taking care of my family. I don't want to be a selfish narcissist, but I also don't need to run myself completely into the ground until I destroy myself spiritually, emotionally, or physically. I want to be a good steward of my health, spirit, and mind. That is a gift to my family.

When I Am Extremely Sleep Deprived

If I am losing a lot of cognitive function and am having trouble treating my family with love and respect because of severe sleep deprivation, and there is not a big emergency keeping me up, I can respectfully ask for help from my husband, children (if they are old enough), or extended family. I can even hire a sitter so I can get the rest I need. If I know it is not safe for me to drive, I need to let another responsible adult or my husband know that I am not okay at the moment. I don't want to risk my life or the lives of my children or others simply because I don't think I should ask for help. All of us need help at times. There is peace in my being able to humbly admit that I am human and accept that I have needs at times.

When I Need Time with God Desperately

When I see that I am snapping at my family or giving in to fear, worry, anger, discouragement, or depression, these are signals I need to notice quickly. As soon as those negative thoughts and temptations begin to flare up, I need to ask myself questions like these:

- How has my time with God been going lately?
- Have I been praying for my own needs?
- Am I listening to God right now?
- What can I do to rest in His love more?
- Do I need to confess any sin?
- What can I praise and thank God for today?

If I have young babies, I can try to do my quiet time when they have nap time or while they are nursing/bottle-feeding. If my children are old enough to understand, I can ask them to play quietly in another room, or I can even let them watch a thirty-minute wholesome video while I take time to reconnect and recharge with God. I might be able to wake up before everyone else and squeeze in a few minutes with God alone. I can also sing praises to God throughout the day even with my children around. I can listen to Scripture or solid Bible-teaching sermons while I am cleaning the house. I can pray when I am driving to work. Sometimes having a quiet time with God takes a bit of creativity depending on my season in life.

I cannot afford to skip time with God any more than I could afford to go for days without eating food. He is my lifeline! He is my only spiritual power source! I have to make time for Him and His Word. I can't spiritually starve myself and be a godly wife and mom. It just is not possible. God created our bodies to have specific daily needs. He also created our souls to have specific daily spiritual needs.

When I Am Not in a Safe Frame of Mind to Be with Others

If I am thinking about hurting myself, my husband, my children, or others—I should not stay alone and try to handle this by myself. I need to reach out for help to 911, my husband (if appropriate), a trusted pastor, my doctor, a godly counselor, a reliable friend, or a family member. If I am a danger to others or myself, I need to get help as soon as possible to protect my family and myself. My first priority must be to do no harm to my family or myself (Rom. 13:10).

When I Am Suffering from Uncontrolled Mental Illness

If I am experiencing severe depression, mania, schizophrenia, bipolar disorder, hallucinations, disassociation, or any other major mental health issue, and I am not in my right state of mind, I need to reach out for trustworthy help right away and not try to handle things on my own. I need a responsible, clear-thinking adult to be with me. I will have to humble myself and not trust my own judgment at the moment. I don't need to try to make important decisions until I am better. I may need to depend on my husband's wisdom or a trusted family member or counselor's wisdom until I am in my right mind again. I may even need help from an experienced doctor.

When I Am Suffering from Spiritual Oppression

Perhaps I am in such terrible condition spiritually that I can't function, or I have such a deep spiritual stronghold that I am completely tied up in severe anxiety, depression, suicidal thoughts, or ideas of self-harm. That is another time when I need to reach out for help. I should not believe the lies of the enemy that "no one understands," "I shouldn't bother anyone with my problems," or "I am beyond God's help." There are believers who are strong prayer warriors who can pray with people who are dealing with major spiritual warfare and strongholds to help them find God's healing.

Thankfully, even if you don't have strong prayer warriors in your life, you can ask God to help you. You can pray for God to open your eyes to any lies and wrong thinking you may have, and you can ask God to heal you and to help you see His truth. You can ask Him to set you free from anything that is not of Him, and you can decide to trust Him. God can spiritually heal those who call on Him in faith and who earnestly seek Him! Jesus loves to set the captives free. You may even want to read about spiritual warfare to learn to pray about things like this. Perhaps you could search "spiritual warfare" at www.desiringgod .org, at www.radical.net, or other trusted resources that align with biblical truth.

We will be examining our hearts for oppressive lies in chapter 3, which may be a big help with spiritual warfare as well.

WHY I BELIEVED "I CAN'T HAVE NEEDS" —SARAH'S STORY AND INSIGHTS

My old way of thinking was about "righteously" refusing to have needs, emotions, or demands. That way of living made me really sick emotionally, physically, and spiritually. To receive nothing good and only receive bad (usually from lies I believed) truly made me toxic. I felt I should have enough faith to be "above struggles and emotions" myself, even though I would never say anyone else should be. I was always the first one to comfort hurting people, because I knew the pain of trying to go through things alone and felt no one should ever have to do that (except for me). My definition of being humble was "not needing, asking, or demanding." That's for others.

These statements describe my old way of thinking:

· I believed that because Jesus saved me I should be able to obey all His commandments in my own strength.
· I tried to please God without faith.
· I did not receive His love, grace, forgiveness, power, and mercy. I had no idea that all the good qualities mentioned about Him could somehow be directed to include me, too.
· I felt totally blocked by anyone who disagreed or said no to me, but I felt I was not allowed to say no or to disagree with them.
· My feelings were my only source of "truth."
· My biggest fears were about being a burden, a failure, and a demanding person.

Behind the false humility was pride, saving myself, and being wise in my own eyes. I felt pride that I was following the "rules," astonishment when I couldn't follow the rules on my own. I was a Christian! How could I fail God like this? So I attacked and punished myself, trying to help God with His disappointment in me. I tried harder until I literally couldn't try anymore. Then I sank into a deep depression and couldn't be pulled out.

Here's how Jesus responded to false humility/pride:

He came to Simon Peter, who said to him, "Lord, are you going to wash my feet?"

Jesus replied, "You do not realize now what I am doing, but later you will understand."

"No," said Peter, "you shall never wash my feet."

Jesus answered, "Unless I wash you, you have no part with me."

"Then, Lord," Simon Peter replied, "not just my feet but my hands and my head as well!"

Jesus answered, "Those who have had a bath need only to wash their feet; their whole body is clean." (John 13:6–10)

Faith is the ability to receive from God:

- He really is here with me and will never leave me.
- I can ask for help from God and receive it.
- God knows I need things and wants me to ask for what I need.
- It is not wrong or rude to have needs and desires and to ask for things from God and from people.

SOME WAYS I CAN PUT ON MY OXYGEN MASK

"Putting on my oxygen mask" should be a normal part of my life with my children. I can structure our family time and priorities to be sure that my children's needs are met and that I try to meet my own needs, too, in most situations.

Taking Care of My Physical Needs

No one else can take a nap for me, eat nutritious food for me, or take a walk for me. I might have to change my priorities. Perhaps the laundry can wait. The floors and bathrooms might be dirty longer than they used to be at certain seasons of life.

Maybe I can trade babysitting with a friend. My husband might be willing to help with some of the household chores or to take the children out for a bit to do something fun so that I can rest—especially if I ask him respectfully. I might find a way that works for me to plan and cook nutritious meals ahead of time on the weekends so I just have to warm things up quickly in the microwave during the week.

Meals don't have to be super fancy or complicated to be healthy and delicious.

I may need to adjust my expectations at certain times. Maybe a thirty-minute simple meal of spaghetti with ground turkey and whole grain pasta, some garlic toast, and a bag of salad is fine. Maybe I don't need to spend two hours on one meal. Or I may be able to teach my children as they get older to help me cook until they are able to take over some of the cooking. That is a skill they will need in the future. It may even be a lot of fun to cook together. Those are wonderful memories we can make together.

> "Part of being a peaceful mom is
> that I receive God's . . . care for me."

I can pray for God's wisdom about how I can take good care of my children and family and also be a good steward of the life and body He has entrusted to me. Everything is to ultimately glorify God. Part of the way God cares for me is that He wants to provide for my needs. I think this is beautifully illustrated in Psalm 23 when David describes God as his loving Shepherd. Many of us have heard this psalm. But I want to really digest it and absorb the care God freely provides for me and learn to live it every day.

Am I receiving all of His provision for me? Part of being a peaceful mom is that I receive God's shepherding and care for me. I can't have the good things He offers me if I fight Him or refuse to receive His gifts. When I receive what He provides, then I am able to have God's peace in my own heart and mind.

> The LORD is my shepherd, I lack nothing.
>> He makes me lie down in green pastures,
>> he leads me beside quiet waters,
>> he refreshes my soul.

He guides me along the right paths
for his name's sake. (Ps. 23:1–3)

I also want to note that just because my flesh is weak because my physical needs haven't been met, that doesn't mean I have a free pass to sin. Even if I am exhausted, hormonal, sick, or in pain, God still desires me to walk in obedience to Him. He can even give me His power so I can obey Him as I allow Him to have control. Here is some encouragement for us as we face such situations:

He said to me, "My grace is sufficient for you, for my power is made perfect in weakness." Therefore I will boast all the more gladly about my weaknesses, so that Christ's power may rest on me. That is why, for Christ's sake, I delight in weaknesses, in insults, in hardships, in persecutions, in difficulties. For when I am weak, then I am strong. (2 Cor. 12:9–10)

Turning Away from Any Spiritual Danger

One of the greatest ways I can put on my oxygen mask and protect my own spiritual health is to ask God to show me any sin in my life. Sin is anything that "misses the mark." It is an archery term. If I miss the target by half an inch, it is a sin. If I miss it by fifty feet, it is also a sin. Anything in my thinking and in my life that misses the mark of God's standard of total perfection and holiness is sin.

Repentance is a huge key to peace.

It is critical that I see this and turn away from every kind of disobedience to God, embracing His ways instead. True repentance means that I do a one-eighty—that I turn from going down the wrong path and turn back to God. It is not just saying I was wrong while I continue in the same direction. I must turn around and head the other way. A key to being a peaceful mom is to be willing to examine my life with God's help, by the light of His Word, and to repent from every single thing He shows me that grieves Him. When I get rid of sin and embrace God's holiness, His peace fills my heart and mind.

Cutting Out Nonessentials

Our culture often equates a person's level of busyness with that person having great value. But God does not think this way. He has an eternal perspective. When I am extremely busy and overscheduled, the first thing to go is my time with God. That is something I cannot afford to miss!

> A woman named Martha opened her home to [Jesus]. She had a sister called Mary, who sat at the Lord's feet listening to what he said. But Martha was distracted by all the preparations that had to be made. She came to him and asked, "Lord, don't you care that my sister has left me to do the work by myself? Tell her to help me!"
>
> "Martha, Martha," the Lord answered, "you are worried and upset about many things, but few things are needed—or indeed only one. Mary has chosen what is better, and it will not be taken away from her." (Luke 10:38–42)

Prayer, reading God's Word, and fellowshiping with Him are my sources of power for living the life God desires me to live. If I don't nourish my soul, I become spiritually anemic and weak. That is not a blessing to anyone. Truly, all I can do when I am operating in my flesh is cause destruction and dysfunction in all of my relationships.

The next thing I sacrifice when I am too busy is the time I could use to build relationships with family and others. If I am busy enough, it is all I can do to barely survive and try to get only the most urgent things taken care of. Sadly, I then miss out on the most important things for my soul and for other people—intimacy, relationship, and connection. These are the things that will ultimately last forever and that will matter most when this short life is over.

I believe I must be rather ruthless in cutting even good things from my schedule and my life that would interfere with the time I need for the most important things. This requires constant vigilance, much like tending a garden and pulling out the weeds as soon as they spring up. If I need to have a less stressful job, a shorter commute, or fewer hours at my job—maybe those are needed changes about which I can fervently pray and also discuss with my husband, if I am married.

Perhaps I need to consider releasing some of my volunteer positions, giving up my screen time, or letting go of my hobbies in order to have the time I need with God and with my family. I may even need to prayerfully consider how much time I am spending in ministry to see if I am overextending myself and need to cut back.

One sign that I may be too involved in ministering to others outside my family is if my husband is not supportive of what I am doing. Another sign might be if I am constantly overwhelmed, resentful, or exhausted. Or I may realize I believe that people need me more than they need God. These things can be red flags that I need to stop and really listen to God.

If a particular ministry is God's will for me, He can change my husband's heart so that he will be in favor of me doing that ministry—even if he is not a believer. If God doesn't change my husband's heart, that may be because God doesn't want me involved in that activity at this time. If God wants me involved in ministry, it will be all about His power working in and through me, not my own strength. I am not the key to any ministry. Jesus is.

If I am so busy serving God and trying to minister to others that I am not sitting at Jesus's feet and taking the time I need to grow in my own faith, I am in serious trouble. It is better for me to slow down, focus on my own walk with Christ, and be sure I am in God's will than to continue charging forward at one hundred miles per hour without God. Any ministry I attempt to do in my own strength and wisdom will not bring real fruit for God's kingdom. In fact, it may do more spiritual harm than good in others' lives. It is not my job to be the entire kingdom of God. My job is only to do the assignments God gives to me, and He will give me the power to do each of them.

> ## Sacrifice of good things can sometimes be necessary so I can focus on the best things.

Something else I personally am convicted about is how much stuff we have. It takes a crazy amount of time to clean and organize a lot of possessions. What a beautiful thing to give more of the things we don't need to people who could use them and enjoy them. That blesses them, and it blesses us! They have something they needed, and we can spend less time cleaning and straightening so that we can focus more on God and people. That is a win-win.

Of course, I would discuss this with my husband and be sure he is on board before I start giving away any of his things or making radical changes for the family. My husband doesn't like sudden, major changes the way I do. He and our children appreciate more gradual changes. If he isn't as gung ho about living with less stuff, I can be patient and do what I can to pare down my personal possessions as I trust God to work in my husband's heart on these issues. As I get rid of the time wasters and space wasters in my life, I have more time and space to fill with the things of God. That is a key to being a peaceful mom.

Charles Hummel put it this way in his book *The Tyranny of the Urgent*:

> An experienced factory manager once said to me, "Your greatest danger is letting the urgent things crowd out the important." He didn't realize how hard his advice hit. It has often

returned to haunt and rebuke me by raising the critical problem of priorities.[1]

Creating Time with God

This is not optional for me. I need time with God and His Word as desperately as I need oxygen to breathe. I know I tend to think, "I don't have time to spend hours with God today because of all I have to do." But if I am running around like crazy and rushing, trying to do a lot for God and my family, it may all be useless if I am not filled up to overflowing with Christ. I must have something worthwhile inside me if I am to give to everyone else.

> But when you pray, go into your room, close the door and pray to your Father, who is unseen. Then your Father, who sees what is done in secret, will reward you. (Matt. 6:6)

> Take my yoke upon you and learn from me, for I am gentle and humble in heart, and you will find rest for your souls. For my yoke is easy and my burden is light. (Matt. 11:29–30)

Even if I am in a stage of life where my children are young, I am not sleeping much, and my time is limited, if I can carve out ten to fifteen minutes per day to read the Bible, it will bless me and my family. Perhaps I can do my quiet time while my children have nap time or when I am nursing or bottle-feeding my baby. I can also memorize a Scripture verse or passage each week and meditate on it by placing it near the kitchen sink or on the dashboard of my car. It is important for my children to know that Mom needs time alone with God and to teach them to respect that time by only interrupting if there is an emergency.

I can also sing praises to God throughout the day even with my children around. I can listen to Scripture or solid Bible-teaching sermons while I am cleaning the house. I can pray and sing praises or listen to the Bible on an app when I am driving to work. I might talk with my children about God and His creation while we are walking. I can start a list of things I am thankful for. Maybe I could include them in my Bible reading and prayer times—have them act out the Bible story I'm reading, ask them to pray for me, recruit them to help me find things to be thankful for.

> "I need time with God and
> His Word as desperately as I
> need oxygen to breathe."

I hear from women sometimes who want God's peace without God and without spending time with Him. They say they don't have time to read the Bible or to pray. That won't work! The fact that I abide in Christ is the main key to being a peaceful mom! It's what helps me keep myself off the throne and let God be God over my life. If I don't continually feed on His Word and His presence, I will quickly slip other things onto the throne in my heart, and then I will certainly crash and burn.

To be a peaceful mom without God would be like trying to take a three-thousand-mile trip across the country in a car with no gas in the tank. It is exhausting to push a car even a few feet. I need Jesus in my life to give me the power I need, just like a car needs gas to have power.

The best way I know to beef up my relationship with Christ is to focus on these kinds of activities:

- Praising Him for His character with words in my heart, out loud, and with singing (even with my children)
- Thanking Him for all the countless blessings in my life
- Confessing any sinful motives, thoughts, words, or actions in my life
- Inviting God to show me sins I may not be able to see

- Sharing any needs I have or that others have and entrusting each one to God's loving care
- Yielding myself fully to His lordship
- Seeking His greatest glory and His perfect will and nothing but His will in my life
- Meditating on His Word and seeking to learn all I can of His ways
- Listening and being open to His voice and quick to respond to His correction or instruction

As I allow God to fill me up with His presence, His truth, His Spirit, and His power, I have the ability to be a peaceful mom no matter what my circumstances may be.

MY PRIORITIES WERE NOT RIGHT —JANELLE'S STORY

I love being a mother and a wife, but both these roles have caused me to neglect myself at times. I work as a nurse, so my instinct is to put others first. This goes for at work and at home. It became more evident how much I was putting others first when I became a mom. The role was so overwhelming that I became very depressed in the first year after our son was born. I praise God for walking with me during this dark time because He was the only reason that I got through it.

I gave everything to my son and started to become so exhausted with what was required of me that I started to neglect my husband. It shocked me one day when he said to me, "You love him more than me." At first I was thinking, "You must be crazy. This little person will die if I do not care for him," but it woke me up and made me start to pray to God to help me with this problem.

I cannot say that it got better right away, but awareness of a problem is the first step. God has been so faithful to show me little opportunities to balance out my life. My health also suffered because I neglected it and stopped exercising and would eat to comfort my negative feelings. I cried out to God for help and to show me how I can gain back my energy. I was tired of feeling exhausted at the end of the day, and I had no energy to study my Bible or exercise. I gained weight and started to lose a lot of my hair. God is giving me strength to be consistent in the small steps that I am taking now to put balance in my life so that I can take larger steps down the road.

How to Evaluate Whether I'm Taking Good Care of Myself

Let's take a peek at how you are doing lately with putting on your own oxygen mask first. Here are some questions to consider:

Am I taking good care of my physical body?
- What healthy food might I eat this week?
- What junk food could I cut out of my diet?
- What could I do differently to get the sleep I need?
- What medical problems do I have that may hinder me from being the woman, wife, and mom God desires me to be? Have I prayed for God's wisdom, healing, and discernment? How might I need to address those in a way that honors God?

Am I taking good care of myself spiritually?
- What do I need to do to get my time in with God?
- What is the fruit of my life? Doubt, anxiety, fear, and bitterness or peace, joy, and fulfillment?
- How could I use my time with God and my time throughout the day more productively?

- What things do I know God wants me to do that I am not doing?
- Is my spiritual walk balanced? Do I only ask God for things I want, or do I have a well-rounded relationship with Him where I praise and thank Him, confess my sins, and listen, as well?
- In what areas might I be holding back and not trusting God completely?

I don't have to be everything to everyone. In fact, I can't do it. It is not possible. Even if it were possible for me to do everything that my family and other people want me to do, it would not be wise. My job is only to do the things God has called me to do. Sometimes people may ask me to do things, but if God is not in it, I may have to politely say no.

When I can accept my limitations and recognize that I need to take care of myself properly so that I can meet appropriate needs my family has, that is a big key to being a peaceful mom. Another key is that I am willing to make the time to receive all that God has for me each day. Peace and rest in Christ come as a result of my commitment to walk in complete obedience and holiness. When I humble myself in this way before God, Jesus gives me His supernatural power to live the holy life He longs for me to live. This leads to contentment and tranquility in my heart.

A Peaceful Mom's Prayer

Lord,

Please help me evaluate if I am so busy that I am ignoring You and my family. Give me Your wisdom to see if there is anything You want me to cut out of my life that may be strangling me physically, emotionally, or spiritually and stunting my growth. Prune me. Refine me. Prepare me to be much more fruitful for You. I am willing to let go of anything that You say needs to go. Help me hold all things loosely but Jesus. Help me have Your wisdom to be a godly steward of the priceless body and life You have provided for me. Let my motives be only for Your glory and to bless those I love. Let me especially find ways to take the time I need to grow in Christ so that, from Your abundance, I might minister to my family and others.

Amen!

Correcting Skewed Beliefs

We take captive every thought to make it obedient to Christ.
(2 Corinthians 10:5)

My parents always considered every person to be of equal worth and value, no matter where those people were from, what their gender was, or what their skin color might be. We had friends from many nationalities and of many colors in the neighborhood where I grew up near Pittsburgh, Pennsylvania. I assumed that everyone thought like my parents did.

I absorbed the message my parents taught me through their example. Didn't question it. In fact, I never even could have imagined anyone thinking any other way. Messages about important topics like this seem to stick with children for a long time. I'm so thankful for the godly example my parents set in this and many other areas.

Just as my parents influenced me, my thoughts and beliefs are "contagious" to my children. They tend to absorb my views about almost everything in this world. I don't have to consciously teach these things to them or even express them out loud. Children are extremely perceptive and almost impossible to fool. They see past what I say and latch on to what I really believe in my heart, and then they tend to adopt my way of thinking about things. My belief system, attitudes, motives, speech, and behavior define "normal" for them in many ways.

"My thoughts and beliefs are 'contagious' to my children."

As my children mature, they will probably start to question the things I believe. That is a painful thing for me as a mom sometimes, but it is an important step as my children move from just mimicking my example to deciding what they will believe for themselves. Still, my example will continue to influence them for the rest of their lives, even when I am no longer with them. They will remember what was important to me. They will remember my words and priorities. They may choose to pattern their lives after my example, or they may rebel against it. If I am going to use this gift and position in a way that honors God and greatly blesses my children, I must be intentional about uncovering what I truly believe and choosing how I live.

MY CORE BELIEFS

Each of us has a core set of beliefs. We developed these when we were growing up, as we were influenced by our parents, church leaders, schoolteachers, the media, our peers, and our experiences. We continue to refine these deep beliefs even in adulthood. My core beliefs or fixed beliefs are the basic ideas upon which I build my life. They are deeply held convictions about God, relationships, masculinity, femininity, marriage, society, family, self, and other critical concepts about my identity and personhood. These beliefs are the things I hold to be true. I make the most important decisions in my life based on my understanding of these concepts.

My core beliefs determine how I think about things such as these:

- Sense of self
- Understanding of how to build healthy relationships
- Understanding of who God is and what His character is like
- Expectations about how marriage and family are supposed to function
- Expectations about how to be a productive member of society
- Understanding of what it means to be a woman
- Understanding of what masculinity should be
- Identity and sense of worth
- Understanding of other people's worth
- Ideas about what love should look like
- Ability to stand up for myself
- Morals, convictions, and priorities
- Greatest dreams and goals

These core beliefs determine the trajectory of my life and influence my children. Many of these beliefs are so ingrained in my thinking that it may be difficult or painful for me to even imagine questioning the validity of them. It may feel like they are carved in stone. But it is essential for me to test my core beliefs against the truth of God's Word to be sure I am building my life on truth rather than lies.

How Our Beliefs Get Skewed

One Sunday morning, my twin sister and I were getting ready for church. We were standing at the top of the stairs when she asked me to buckle her sandals for her. I said, "You're five years old! Buckle your own sandals." She said she couldn't because her tights were too tight. She started hanging on me, begging me to buckle her sandals for her. I pushed her away, not realizing how close we were to the staircase. I can still remember the look of horror on her face as she fell backward down the stairs. I ran to my room and hid in my closet.

My father was *not* happy. I have never been in so much trouble in all my life. Daddy told me that I should have checked on my sister and that she could have died because I pushed her down the stairs. I never did that again! I got the message that I should not push people, especially at the top of the stairs. I also got the message that if I do hurt someone, I should check to be sure that person is okay and should get help if needed.

But I got another message that my parents didn't intend for me to learn. I told myself, "I can never tell anyone no when I'm asked for help. I have to always help people even if I don't want to, or they could die." Of course, no one else knew that was what I was thinking.

> "Core beliefs determine the trajectory of my life and influence my children."

Fast-forward to third grade on the playground. My twin sister, a friend, and I were on top of the monkey bars. Suddenly, two boys from our class started coming up the monkey bars to try to get us. I yelled to the girls, "Jump!" We all jumped. I was totally fine. My sister sprained her ankle. Our friend broke her leg. I felt *so* guilty and responsible. I believed it was completely my fault that my sister and our friend were hurt so badly. After all, I was the one who said to jump. They did what I said to do. I quickly decided that I wished I could have a broken leg too.

I felt I deserved to be hurt because it was my idea for us to jump. Eventually, I even started to have real pain in my legs. I wanted to be in a wheelchair. Maybe that would have helped me not feel so guilty. I couldn't bear the weight of the responsibility I felt. I couldn't really articulate all of this to my parents at the time, so they didn't know what all was going on in my mind. All they knew was that I was trying to hurt myself and that I wanted a broken leg, and it didn't make any sense to them at all.

After these two incidents—and with the addition of some sermons I interpreted to mean, "If *you* don't witness to people, they are going to hell and it is your fault"—I developed a very strong core belief. I thought I heard that I was truly responsible for other people, their lives, their decisions, and their situations. I even believed I was responsible to fix famines and to be sure all the people in the world had food to eat. I cried about that issue every night when I was eight years old. This was my fault, and I needed to fix it, but I couldn't. The guilt was overwhelming. I saw my responsibility as huge and God as very small.

This wrong core belief adversely impacted me for decades and contributed greatly to my compulsion to try to control other people. It hurt my marriage, my children, and my other relationships. I believed it was my duty and responsibility to make other people do what was best, to protect them, and to make sure things turned out correctly. Other people did not appreciate or agree with this belief of mine, so I wrote them off as being "wrong." It also caused me to depend on myself rather than on God. I subconsciously believed I carried some of God's sovereignty on myself. This was not something I could just easily "switch off." To change a core belief takes a lot of purposeful effort, prayer, and the power of the Holy Spirit.

Unfortunately, sometimes we all receive information that is not true, either because people teach us wrong information or because we misunderstand important issues. The more dysfunctional our environment, the more skewed our understanding tends to be. If I absorb lies and build my life on wrong beliefs, my life has a faulty spiritual foundation. Spiritual foundations are as important as physical foundations for buildings. If I build without a solid foundation, my life will eventually begin to crumble under the weight of stress and storms (Matt. 7:24–27).

There are countless ways that we can develop skewed beliefs. None of us are exempt from this, even if we have very godly parents. The majority of our skewed thinking seems to happen in childhood and carry into adulthood, although we can certainly still allow our beliefs to be skewed as adults as well.

Here some ways I might have developed wrong thinking as a child:

- My parents or a teacher may have tried to teach me the truth about a concept, but I misunderstood it and built my life on that misunderstanding.
- I may have been indoctrinated with lies at home or at school.
- My parents may have had wrong thinking in their own lives, and I absorbed their ideas and assumed they were true.
- I may have misheard or misunderstood a pastor's sermon.
- I may have gone to a church where the truth was present but rather muddled.
- I may have gone to a church where there was false teaching.
- I may not have had access to the Bible or sound biblical teaching, so I made up my own ideas about certain topics.
- I may have read the Bible but misunderstood parts of it.
- I may have absorbed wrong thinking from books, the media, or friends.
- I may not have had a strong discipleship relationship to help me grow in my faith.

The scary thing is that I wouldn't have known that my thinking was wrong. If I knew it was wrong, I wouldn't have kept that idea and built my life on it. Usually, we are blind to our own skewed thinking. We deceive ourselves. If the adults we trusted had this kind of thinking, it will seem very normal. But even if no one else thinks the way we do, our thinking makes sense to us and seems right to us. We may not know how to change it or even think we can change it.

> All a person's ways seem pure to them,
>   but motives are weighed by the Lord. (Prov. 16:2)

UNDERSTANDING SKEWED BELIEFS —BETH'S INSIGHTS

Developing skewed beliefs is something all kids do. Whether someone feeds them lies on purpose or not, no matter how good a job we try to do, and no matter how much we try to protect them, this will happen to some degree. The bottom line is they all still need redemption, the cross, to die to self, and to experience a resurrected life with Jesus and the Holy Spirit.

How to Recognize Skewed Beliefs

There are ways, thankfully, to recognize lies in our core beliefs. The key is that I have to be willing to compare all the things I think to the truth and invite God to help me discern between lies and truth. This can be scary and uncomfortable. Many people balk at doing this necessary heart work. But if I don't address my wrong thinking, I will stay very stuck.

"The only source of absolute truth is the Bible."

The only source of absolute truth is the Bible. I am walking in darkness if I go to any other source to evaluate my beliefs. When I build my life on wrong thoughts, I am building on sinking sand rather than on the solid rock of Christ and His Word. I must purposely and carefully evaluate all my own deepest beliefs against the truth of the Bible, with the help of the Holy Spirit. Anything that does not hold up to Scripture has to go.

This process does require that I know the Bible and that I know how to handle it rightly. If I don't know the Bible very well, there are many resources to help me study it. (Please see appendix C.) It would be ideal for me to have a Bible-teaching, Bible-living pastor and church where I can grow and learn. If possible, it can also be helpful to have a trusted, godly, biblical teacher or mentor to help me learn and grow in my understanding. But everything any human teacher says has to pass the test of whether it agrees with the Bible. Above all, I need to have God's Spirit.

If I continue to build my life on lies rather than truth, over time I will reap the consequences of my wrong or sinful thoughts in these forms:

- Lack of fellowship with Christ (Eph. 4:30)
- Absence of the fruit of the Spirit (Gal. 5:22–23)
- Dysfunctional relationships with others (Gal. 5:18–21)
- Lack of spiritual appetite and power (1 Thess. 5:19)
- Prayerlessness (Isa. 43:22)
- Lack of desire for God (Rom. 3:10–18)
- Stress, anxiety, fear, sinful thoughts, hatred, or bitterness (Ps. 139:23–24; 1 Cor. 11:30)
- Physical illness at times (Ps. 38:3)
- Wrong motives that lead to sinful thoughts, words, and actions (Prov. 21:2)

When I build on lies, I will see the fruit of my sinful nature, not the fruit of God. When I build on God's truth, there is peace because His Spirit is with me and is empowering me. A key to being a peaceful mom is to have my life governed by the Spirit of God and built on truth.

> The mind governed by the flesh is death, but the mind governed by the Spirit is life and peace. (Rom. 8:6)

I can't just assume that I think rightly about everything. I need to be willing to take a sweeping spiritual inventory of myself fairly often and be willing to get rid of any thought or belief that is not biblical. God wants to cleanse my thought life. This is kind of a spiritual "spring-cleaning." As I allow God to help me clean house in my mind, He gives me the ability to know His will for me in greater detail.

> Do not conform to the pattern of this world, but be transformed by the renewing of your mind. Then you will be able to test and approve what God's will is—his good, pleasing and perfect will. (Rom. 12:2)

In fact, if God has shown me something that is His will for me and I don't obey Him, I will have a hard time discerning God's will after that. I must go back to the last thing I did hear from God about what He wanted me to do and obey that. Then when I am walking in obedience and fellowship with the Lord again, He will show me more of His will. He doesn't reveal more of His will to those who refuse to obey the part of His will they already know.

How to Correct Our Beliefs

The Bible can also be used as a sword to deflect Satan's lies. Jesus set an example in this. When Satan tempted Him, He rightly applied God's Word to strike down the temptation to wrong thinking and to walk in obedience to God. He did not absorb Satan's lies. He didn't allow them to take root in his heart. He discerned truth from lies and didn't welcome anything that was not true into His thinking.

> ## "What I say to myself is very important."

The Bible is also the surgeon's scalpel that God will use in my life to precisely and skillfully excise sinful, destructive thoughts that have taken root. My willingness to get rid of wrong thinking, even if it's painful at first to do so, and to build my life on God's truth alone leads to much peace in my mind and soul.

I know I personally have an almost constant stream of internal dialogue going on every waking moment. That is a lot of thinking to evaluate. It may be a bit overwhelming when I first begin to monitor my thoughts and motives to see how often negative, wrong, or sinful thoughts are percolating in my mind. But what I say to myself is very important, and this discipline of reigning in my thoughts is crucial for me to allow God to transform my thinking.

TAKING MY THOUGHTS CAPTIVE

I can stop myself when I have a questionable thought. Often the first clue will be negative feelings—anxiety, frustration, disappointment, or fear—surrounding that particular thought. So I bring my thoughts to God in prayer. For some women, journaling is a great way to process their thoughts in prayer. For others, speaking into a recording device may be helpful. Others may just prefer to pray out loud or silently.

The first step is to ask God to help us recognize our deepest thoughts and hidden motives. I can't address a problem that I don't know exists. Once I see the wrong thinking or a potential tempting thought, I can ask God to help me determine whether that thought is of Him or of the enemy—because those are the only two origins of spiritual thoughts (Rom. 8:5–8; Eph. 2:1–3). Then I prayerfully compare my thoughts to Scripture. This is called testing the spirits (1 John 4:1). I only want to keep thoughts that agree with and come from God.

Then I ask God to help me trash any wrong ideas or temptations. Once the wrong thoughts are gone, I purposely turn to the Bible and the Holy Spirit to help me replace my wrong thinking with God's right thinking. This is how He transforms and renews my mind. It is not enough to stop the wrong thinking and to just say, "I won't think about that anymore." I must replace the sinful, wrong thoughts with holy,

right thoughts. Then I apply those right thoughts to my life in obedience to Christ as Lord. I open the door of my mind and heart to invite
God to take control so He can change and heal me.

Some scriptural keys to taking my thoughts captive for Christ include these:

> You will keep in perfect peace
>   those whose minds are steadfast,
>   because they trust in you. (Isa. 26:3)

> Jesus said, "If you hold to my teaching, you are really my disci-
> ples. Then you will know the truth, and the truth will set you
> free." (John 8:31–32)

> Finally, brothers and sisters, whatever is true, whatever is noble,
> whatever is right, whatever is pure, whatever is lovely, whatever
> is admirable—if anything is excellent or praiseworthy—think
> about such things. (Phil. 4:8)

> Submit yourselves, then, to God. Resist the devil, and he will
> flee from you. (James 4:7)

When I know God and His truth, I have His peace in every area of
my life because I have freedom in Jesus.

I would encourage you to take some time this week to look through
the charts on the coming pages and check (or write down) which ones
you believe may apply to you. Some of these lies are more subconscious
than conscious, so please ask God for His discernment and for His help
in examining the fixed beliefs you may have and correcting anything
that is not in line with God's Word. Then you can work to apply God's
truth to your own life.

Some Common Lies About God

Lie	God's Truth	Bible References
He is evil.	He is completely good.	Psalm 86:5
He is out to get me.	He is for me.	Jeremiah 29:11
I have to earn His love. Jesus's work on the cross was not enough.	Jesus's work on the cross was enough to make me right with God. I can't earn His love, but I can receive His grace and provision for me.	Ephesians 2:8–10
He is holding out on me.	He wants the best for me and has proven He will withhold no good thing from me.	Romans 8:32
His commands are oppressive.	His commands bring real freedom, peace, and rest.	Matthew 11:28–30 John 8:32
He is small and wimpy.	God has all the authority and power in the universe.	Job 42:2 Colossians 1:16
He is tempting me.	God can't tempt anyone.	James 1:13–15
He can't or won't help me.	God wants to help me if I will seek Him above all else.	Luke 11:13 John 4:10 1 Peter 5:7
He is not sovereign.	God is sovereign.	2 Chronicles 20:6 Psalm 135:6 Daniel 4:35 John 6:44 Ephesians 1:5

Lie	God's Truth	Bible References
God is a tyrant, and people are just robots with no choices.	People have responsibility and choices and are accountable to God for them.	Genesis 2:16–17 Deuteronomy 11:26–28 John 1:12 Revelation 3:20
He needs me, or His work can't get done.	God doesn't need me. He can accomplish His work without me, but He wants to use me if I am willing.	Psalm 40:5 Acts 17:24–25
He is not enough for me.	Jesus is more than enough!	2 Corinthians 12:8–10 Philippians 4:10–13, 19
Circumstances are greater than He is.	He is much bigger than any circumstances on earth.	Matthew 8:26 Matthew 19:26 Luke 7:22
His Word is not true or not totally true.	God's Word is completely true and trustworthy.	John 17:17 2 Timothy 3:16 2 Peter 1:20
I can't trust Him.	I can't trust myself but I can trust God!	Psalm 34:8 Proverbs 1:7 Proverbs 3:5–6 John 14:1–3
He is hateful and unloving.	God is the very definition of love.	1 John 4:8, 16
He is not just.	God is completely just.	Nahum 1:3 Revelation 20:12–13 Revelation 21:7–8
He should submit to me.	God owes nothing to me. I owe everything to God, and my proper place is in full submission to Him as Lord.	Isaiah 45:9–12 James 4:7

An interesting observation as I look at most of these lies: they are completely untrue about God, but the statements in the far left column are almost all true about Satan. Satan wants me to believe I can trust him and I should listen to and follow him. But in reality, he is evil and out to get me. He is holding out on me. His words and ways are oppressive. He is wimpy compared to God and can do nothing outside the parameters God gives him. He, not God, is tempting me. He is not sovereign. I can't trust him. When I see rightly through the lens of Scripture, I can see with clarity and wisdom. I learn to recognize and distinguish God's voice from Satan's voice in my mind.

Some Common Lies About Self

Lie	God's Truth	Bible References
My wisdom is better than God's wisdom.	God's wisdom is infinitely superior to human wisdom.	Proverbs 11:2 Proverbs 16:5 Isaiah 55:8–9 1 Corinthians 3:18–20
I am worthless/ugly/unlovable to God.	I am deeply loved and precious in God's sight. I have no good in me on my own, but in Jesus, my old, worthless, sinful self is dead, and now I have a new self in Christ that is beautiful, radiant, and spotless because of His grace to me.	2 Corinthians 5:17 Galatians 2:20 1 Peter 2:9
God's promises apply to other people but not to me. I can't receive God's love.	God's Word applies to everyone, and anyone who wants to receive His love and truth can receive it and follow Him wholeheartedly in obedience.	Matthew 7:21–23 John 3:16 Romans 10:9

Lie	God's Truth	Bible References
I should try to convict others of sin. I am responsible for others' decisions, their choices, and the consequences they experience.	I can lovingly, respectfully, humbly speak to others about their sin, but each person has free will and accountability and is responsible to God for the choices made.	Matthew 7:1–5 Matthew 18:15–17 John 16:7–8
My sin isn't as bad as other people's sin. God will accept my justification for my sin.	All sin is repulsive to God. Any sin separates me from God and requires the blood of Jesus to cover it. There is no goodness in me on my own. God will not accept any justification for any sin in my life.	Luke 13:3 Romans 3:23 Romans 6:1–4, 23 1 John 1:8
God can't forgive me.	There is no sin that is beyond the blood of Jesus if I am willing to repent and turn completely away from sin to Christ.	Psalm 51:17 1 John 1:9
I can't forgive myself.	Sin is ultimately all against God. It is His forgiveness that we need. If He is satisfied that the blood of Christ covers my sin, it would be arrogant of me to say that Jesus's blood is not enough in my eyes to cover my sin and that I can't forgive myself.	Psalm 51:4 Psalm 103:12

Lie	God's Truth	Bible References
I am (or should be) the savior for others or myself. I am sovereign over my life and other people's lives and circumstances. I know best for others, and they need my help.	Jesus alone is the Savior I need. He is sovereign, not me. He has the wisdom people need, not me. He knows best, and I can point others and myself to Him. We all need His help.	Isaiah 5:21 Isaiah 2:22 Psalm 118:8 Proverbs 28:26 Matthew 5:36
I am exempt from God's commands.	I am responsible to God for my sin and for my obedience to Him. I am not exempt.	John 14:22–24 Romans 14:10–12
My emotions are greater than God's Word and more important than God's wisdom. They are my source of absolute truth, not the Bible.	God's Word is the only source of absolute truth. My feelings and emotions can deceive me. I can't depend on my feelings and need to choose to trust the Bible over my emotions or anything else.	Proverbs 3:5–7 John 17:17 2 Timothy 3:16–17
I don't need spiritual nourishment from God and His Word.	I am as dependent on time with God, in His Word, and in fervent prayer for my spiritual strength as I am dependent on food, water, and oxygen for my physical strength.	Matthew 4:4 1 Peter 2:2
I don't need to pray for myself.	I desperately need to pray for myself and ask God to make me more like Christ. Prayer brings me closer to the Lord.	Matthew 6:9–15

Lie	God's Truth	Bible References
I can cherish certain sins and lies in my heart and be fine.	Lies and sin are poisonous to my spiritual well-being, my relationship with God, my relationship with other people, and my body. They all have to go.	Psalm 66:18 Ephesians 4:30 1 John 1:8
I am above having to forgive or give grace. I need to hold on to my bitterness.	God commands me to forgive others when they sin against me so that He will forgive me.	Matthew 6:14–15 Ephesians 4:31–32
I haven't been forgiven much because I don't have much sin in my life and really don't need a Savior. I'm pretty good on my own.	I owe God an incalculable debt because of my sin. We all stand on level ground with one another at the foot of the cross. Only Jesus was good and perfect. Only He can make me or anyone else right with God.	Isaiah 53:6 Isaiah 64:6 Romans 3:23 Romans 6:23
I can't know God.	I can know God if I decide to seek Him with all my heart and come to Him through Jesus.	John 14:6 John 17:2–3 Romans 10:13

Some Common Lies About Others

Lie	God's Truth	Bible References
I am more important than other people. Or: Other people are more important than I am because I am worthless.	Every person was created by God in His image. Every person has great value to God.	Genesis 1:27 Matthew 22:39 Romans 12:3 Philippians 2:3–4

Lie	God's Truth	Bible References
I am justified to sin against people if they don't do what I want them to do or if they hurt me. I should take revenge if I am wronged.	God never gives anyone a free pass to sin. I am responsible to obey God and to treat others as He desires me to treat them. He calls me to love my enemies and to repay evil with good. I may need to set healthy boundaries if someone refuses to repent of sin against me.	Matthew 18:15–17 Romans 12:17–21
People are here to serve me. Or: I am only here to be a slave to people.	We are all to serve Christ wholeheartedly and then to bless and serve others in order to honor Him from a place of great spiritual strength in Christ.	Matthew 20:25–26 Galatians 1:10
I have to avoid conflict at all costs. I can't ever let anyone be upset with me. I must please people and have their approval above all else.	I can seek to avoid unnecessary conflict. I can repent of any sin on my part. I can treat others with honor and dignity. But I can accept that some conflict is unavoidable, and I don't have to be afraid of conflict. My goal is to please Christ above all else, even if others are upset.	Matthew 7:1–5 Matthew 10:28 Matthew 18:15–17 Romans 12:18
Others must never disappoint me.	People will fail me and disappoint me. Only God will never fail me and always be faithful to keep His promises.	Psalm 118:8 Jeremiah 17:5–6

Lie	God's Truth	Bible References
Others should submit to me and do what I want them to do. I should be in charge.	Everyone should submit to Christ above all and do His will. Then I should also submit appropriately to those in positions of God-given authority in my life out of reverence for Christ.	Romans 13:1-2 1 Corinthians 13:4-6
Others are responsible for my emotions, my spiritual growth, my responses, and my choices. I am responsible for other people's emotions, spiritual growth, their responses, and choices.	I am responsible and accountable to God for my own decisions and how I handle my emotions, spiritual growth, responses, and choices.	Matthew 12:35-36 Galatians 5:22
I have to disrespect myself to respect others. Or: I have to disrespect others to respect myself. Or: I can't think rightly about and respect God, others, and myself all at the same time.	God calls me to reverence Him above all else. He calls me to die to my old sinful self and not allow that self to be in control in my life anymore. I have a new life and a new holy self, a new Spirit in Christ. I can think rightly about my new self in Christ and receive all the good things God says about my identity in Christ. I can also rightly respect and honor others out of reverence for Christ.	Matthew 22:38-39 1 Corinthians 13:5 Colossians 2:18-23

Lie	God's Truth	Bible References
Others' feelings don't matter. Or: My feelings don't matter.	God cares about my feelings and emotions. I should care about other people's feelings and emotions and respect them. I should rejoice with those who rejoice and mourn with those who mourn. But feelings are not a source of absolute truth and can't be more important than God in our hearts.	Romans 12:15 1 Corinthians 13:4–8

Lots of these issues require proper balance, biblical understanding, and most of all, the power of the Holy Spirit to illuminate our understanding. If I swing too far one way or the other from a particular truth, I quickly veer into a sinful, destructive mind-set. But if I build my life on a right understanding of God's truth and allow His Spirit to transform and empower me, then I experience real healing, joy, and peace.

> "My goal is that my entire
> life . . . be completely built on
> Christ Jesus and His truth."

The more deeply I am willing to dig into my wrong thinking, the better. This is the lifelong process of being conformed to the image of Christ, called "sanctification." It starts with making my thinking align with God's. My goal is that my entire life and every motive and priority be completely built on Christ Jesus and His truth alone. Nothing else is welcome in my heart and mind.

Let's work through an example together so that you have a chance to practice this discipline.

Example: "I'm Not Good Enough"

First, I ask myself, "Does this thought come from God or from Satan? Is it the truth, or is it a lie?"

Who wants me to focus on this idea? Who would most benefit from me thinking this way? Who would love for me to be discouraged and depressed?

> As it is written: "There is no one righteous, not even one; there is no one who understands; there is no one who seeks God. All have turned away, they have together become worthless; there is no one who does good, not even one." (Rom. 3:10–12)

> For we know that our old self was crucified with him so that the body ruled by sin might be done away with, that we should no longer be slaves to sin. . . . In the same way, count yourselves dead to sin but alive to God in Christ Jesus. (Rom. 6:6, 11)

My old self does not have any good in it. That is true. My sinful nature is only fit for crucifixion, which Jesus has already done for me. My old self is dead because I am in Christ. But is that the whole truth about who I am if I belong to Jesus? Sometimes Satan uses parts of Scripture and twists them to deceive me.

Second, I search the Bible for more clarification on my identity in Christ and pray that God will help me to understand the whole teaching of His Word.

There is much more to Scripture if I will dig into it! I can dig into various topics at www.openbible.info or at www.biblegateway.com and instantly find verses about specific words and topics.

So God created mankind in his own image,
in the image of God he created them;
male and female he created them. (Gen. 1:27)

Yet to all who did receive him, to those who believed in his name, he gave the right to become children of God. (John 1:12)

Therefore, if anyone is in Christ, the new creation has come: The old has gone, the new is here! (2 Cor. 5:17)

I have been crucified with Christ and I no longer live, but Christ lives in me. The life I now live in the body, I live by faith in the Son of God, who loved me and gave himself for me. (Gal. 2:20)

You have taken off your old self with its practices and have put on the new self, which is being renewed in knowledge in the image of its Creator. (Col. 3:9–10)

The whole truth is that originally we were all created in the very image of God. I have worth because God created me and He loves me more than I can imagine. My sin separated me from God and made me unable to be good in the way God designed me to be. Yes, my old sinful self deserved condemnation and death, but God has already crucified my old self with Jesus on the cross (if I belong to Him). He has also provided a new life for me: a new spirit, a new mind, and a new heart.

Third, I prayerfully evaluate what the Bible says versus my thoughts and feelings.

I feel like I am not good enough. That is partly true. On my own I have no good in me because of my sin. Satan would love for me to continue to focus on that so I would be discouraged and paralyzed as a mom. Jesus says that God alone is good (Mark 10:18). Really, it is a pride thing to think that I should be able to be good enough in my own power. This truth requires me to humble myself before God and acknowledge that I have nothing in myself with which I can impress Him or earn His love and favor. Without Jesus, I am a wretched sinner. My best attempts at holiness look like "filthy rags" in the eyes of God (Isa. 64:6).

What I think about greatly impacts my level of peace.

But now, if I am in Christ, He has given me a new Spirit—His Spirit—and a new nature in Him. I can allow God to fill me to overflowing with His goodness. I can study about my new identity and security in Christ and how, as I freely give all of myself to Him, He freely gives all of Himself to me! How I praise God for His goodness and that He is able to completely make up for my weakness and anything I lack. I am a new creation! Woo-hoo!

Everything that belongs to Jesus belongs to me because we are one in Spirit now. I am His temple, and His glory and goodness fill me to overflowing. I now have His character, His Spirit, His power, His holiness, and His right standing with God. I am a child of God. There is no longer any condemnation for me!

My prayer might sound like this:

Lord,

I thank You that even though there is no good in my old self, You have provided Jesus to crucify my old sinful nature and You have given me a new nature in Christ. I choose to die to my old self and live in the power of my new self in Christ today, recognizing that my sinful self is dead with Christ in Your sight. I choose to receive all that You have done on my behalf through Christ's finished work on the cross. Jesus's work is sufficient. Your power is made perfect in my weakness (2 Cor. 12:9). I will move forward today with confidence—not in myself, but in You alone. I will always boast in Jesus and all He has done for me! Amen.

Fourth, I choose to trust God's Word and His higher wisdom as truth and reject my human wisdom and feelings if there is a conflict between the two.

Starting today, I receive God's truth about me from His Word. My old self is dead and buried with Christ. No, I don't have anything good to brag about in myself, but I receive all that Jesus has done and all of His spiritual riches as well as the new life He died to give to me. He is completely good. I will brag on Him! He generously gives me all His goodness and fills my spiritually bankrupt account with His overflowing one. He will transform my heart, mind, and soul to be more and more like Himself. I will rest in His promises and not listen to the half-truths of the Accuser.

TEACHING MY CHILDREN

I can walk my children through these exact same steps, to help them learn to take their thoughts captive for Christ.

Imagine the blessing of learning to do this from a young age so that children can begin to build their fixed beliefs and their lives on the truth of God from early in life. What a priceless legacy for children to have a mom who knows how to help them build their lives on the solid Rock of Christ—who will help them in spiritual battles, who will teach them to discern truth from lies, and who will pray with them and for them! You may want to review the charts from earlier in this chapter about the lies we tend to believe about God. Think about posting them somewhere handy so you and your children can refer to them as needed.

A key to my ability to be a peaceful mom is that I learn the discipline of taking my thoughts captive for Christ and purify my thought life with God's help. My thoughts, motives, fixed beliefs, and priorities determine the foundation of my relationships with God and with other people. My thought life is the greatest spiritual battleground there is. If I will let God help me to get rid of sinful, dangerous thoughts the second I notice the temptation, I can guard my heart and mind.

If I am quick to repent of sin and to seek to obey God, I will discover that I hear His voice more clearly and I have more of His wisdom and greater discernment as I grow in faith. What I focus on in my thoughts greatly impacts my ability to be filled with the Holy Spirit, and therefore my thoughts help to determine my level of peace.

A PEACEFUL MOM'S PRAYER

Lord,

I see some of these destructive tendencies in my own life. I never want to grieve You! Help me throw away any mind-set or approach that doesn't please You. Forgive me for choosing hurtful ways to relate to my children and husband. Help me to get rid of these and to replace them with thinking, motives, and behavior that honor You greatly. Thank You for showing me some things I need to change. Thank You that You will give me the power I need to walk in victory over these things as I continue to seek You with all my heart. Change me. Make me more like Jesus!

Amen.

Taking Responsibility for My Character

*So then, each of us will give an account of ourselves
to God. (Romans 14:12)*

Many in our culture today believe that other people, not themselves, are responsible for their poor behavior. It is an attitude that says, "He hurt me, so now I am justified to lash out at him." In other words, "If he treats me well, I will treat him well. But if anyone mistreats me, I get to hurt him in return, and it is his own fault for pushing me to do it."

I fell prey to this philosophy for a long time. If I felt unloved, sinned against, or ignored by my husband, then I felt I had a right to respond harshly. It is as if I thought God would be totally fine with me sinning against others if I felt hurt or sinned against myself. Obviously, that idea did not come from Scripture.

Our husbands aren't the only ones to take the brunt of our misplaced responsibility. Sometimes we blame our children for our attitudes, words, and actions: "Well, if you didn't make such a mess, I wouldn't have to yell at you about it!" Or, "You should have done what

I told you to do. It's your own fault I have to tell you how stupid you are now."

Sometimes people even blame God for their sinful attitudes and behavior. This is not a new thing. It has been going on for thousands of years.

> The man said, "The woman you put here with me—she gave me some fruit from the tree, and I ate it." (Gen. 3:12)

> A person's own folly leads to their ruin,
>   yet their heart rages against the LORD. (Prov. 19:3)

If I am not able to blame other people or God, then I am going to have to have a radically different approach. It will not be popular in our culture, but this new approach is a big key to being a peaceful mom.

WHO IS RESPONSIBLE FOR MY THOUGHTS AND ACTIONS?

Scripture is clear about who is responsible for what I do and think. (Hint: It's me.)

All throughout the Bible, God holds individuals responsible for their own sinful motives, words, and actions (people such as Adam, Eve, Cain, the people in the time of Noah's flood, Saul, David, Judas, and Peter). Scripture is clear that God is sovereign, but at the same time, there is also a very strong message that people are accountable to Him for their thoughts, motives, words, and actions. The take-home message for me is that I want to be sure I do my part to avoid sinning against God.

If you're still in doubt, let's take a look at just a handful of the verses that talk about our responsibilities.

> I the LORD search the heart
>   and examine the mind,

> to reward each person according to their conduct,
> according to what their deeds deserve. (Jer. 17:10)

Whoever sows to please their flesh, from the flesh will reap destruction; whoever sows to please the Spirit, from the Spirit will reap eternal life. (Gal. 6:8)

When tempted, no one should say, "God is tempting me." For God cannot be tempted by evil, nor does he tempt anyone; but each person is tempted when they are dragged away by their own evil desire and enticed. Then, after desire has conceived, it gives birth to sin; and sin, when it is full-grown, gives birth to death. (James 1:13–15)

My Character Is About Who Controls Me

The Bible says we have two natures (or capacities). There is the sinful nature that each of us was born with—when we live by it, our lives have bad fruit. But there is also the new nature we have in Christ. When it is in charge, our lives have good fruit. Before I come to Christ, I am a slave to sin. But now—I am so thankful to God for this—I have a choice! I don't have to be a slave to sin. I can choose to live out righteousness.

Make a tree good and its fruit will be good, or make a tree bad and its fruit will be bad, for a tree is recognized by its fruit. . . . For the mouth speaks what the heart is full of. A good man brings good things out of the good stored up in him, and an evil man brings evil things out of the evil stored up in him. But I tell you that everyone will have to give account on the day of judgment for every empty word they have spoken. For by your words you will be acquitted, and by your words you will be condemned. (Matt. 12:33–37)

As long as I live in this world, even though I am in Christ now, I can still choose to revert back to my old sinful nature. In God's eyes, if I belong to Jesus, my old sinful nature is dead and buried with Him. However, I still have access to my sinful nature. I can let it jump back up and take over. God keeps my free will intact so that I have the ability to voluntarily follow, love, and obey Him or to rebel against Him. He doesn't want me to be a robot without a choice. That is where the problem begins.

If my flesh governs my life, I have yielded my mind, my motives, my heart, my mouth, all that I have, and all that I do to accomplish the purposes of Satan. I let him speak death through me to my family and to myself. I accuse others. I berate them. I insult them and seek to divide my family and create strife. I am filled with hatred, contempt, and bitterness. I find peace slipping through my fingers as I yell, manipulate, and throw temper tantrums. The things that the enemy whispers to me sound good and right. I happily spew out his words, allowing Satan to use my mouth to destroy those around me. The things God says sound wrong and oppressive when I don't have His Spirit filling me.

"I will listen to and obey the One to whom I belong."

But if the Spirit of God governs my life, I have yielded my mind, my motives, my heart, my mouth, all that I have, and all that I do to accomplish His purposes. I let His Spirit speak life through me to my family and to myself. I build others up. I affirm them. I encourage them. I speak truth to them. I seek to bless them, to create unity, and to promote godly love. I joyfully overflow with God's words, allowing God to use my words to bring healing, light, and hope to those around me. The things that God's still, small voice whispers to me sound good and right. The things Satan says sound wrong and oppressive when Jesus is my Lord.

The voice I hear in my thoughts the most clearly is the one I am closest to. I will listen to and obey the One to whom I belong. The other voice sounds foreign and repulsive to me.

As a peaceful mom, I have the ability to yield control of my life to Satan or to God. But I know that only one of these choices brings sweet peace. I realize that choosing the flesh is never worth it because it destroys my peace and my family's peace. The cost of sin is way too high.

MY RESPONSIBILITY SPIRITUALLY

Simply put, my job is to love God, love others, be filled with His Spirit, and be fully available to Him (Matt. 22:36–40; John 14:21; Gal. 2:20; 5:16). He desires to use my life to point people to Christ, to share His Word, and to demonstrate His glory while I live in total surrender to Him. He wants me to obey Him. He provides His Spirit so I can do what He is asking me to do.

God loves me more than I can fathom. He also chooses to give me purpose and to use me according to His plans for the kingdom. But He doesn't depend on me—as if I will destroy His plans if I mess up and set the whole world on some terrible uncorrectable tilt. No human can thwart God's purposes, thankfully (Isa. 14:27)! His sovereignty and my free will work together in harmony in ways my brain cannot begin to fathom, even when I mess up.

MY SON SHOWED ME GRACE —MY STORY

When our son was about three years old, I lost my patience with him and yelled at him with total lack of self-control. I had been trying to work on my tone of voice with him and was disgusted with myself that I messed up . . . again. I went and sat on the steps where I usually put him in time-out and told him I was putting myself in time-out because I lost my temper. (I am not saying that is what all moms should do, but that is what I did at that time.)

My precious little boy climbed up the steps and sat right beside me. He put his chubby little arm around me. He smiled at me with those beautiful blue eyes and told me that he forgave me. Then he said, "I sit wiff [with] you, Mama." He patted my back, and we sat there together in silence.

Tears streamed down my face and soon turned to sobs while I took in the incredible expression of grace my son gave me. I should have been the one modeling grace for him. God used my sin of lack of self-control to drive home a humbling and unforgettable lesson for me.

God may use my mistakes or sins and even the pain that those things have caused to lead my children into a specific ministry to others who had similar wounds as children. Or He may use the wrong things I have done in the past as a lesson, so that I can share with my children the things not to do in their lives in the future. God can restore "the years the locusts have eaten" in my own life and my children's lives (Joel 2:25).

Even if I do stumble, God can redeem it all for His purposes.

I never want to purposely sin against my children. But if I do stumble, and we all do at times, God can redeem it all for His purposes. It is such a comfort to know that God can and will make up for what I lack in parenting my children. I don't have to be the perfect parent. My husband doesn't have to be the perfect parent. God is the ultimate, perfect Father—how I praise Him for that! That promise brings me such peace of mind as a mom.

Getting Rid of Sin in My Life Is My Responsibility

It is my job to take care of my own sin, to confess it, and to change direction. No matter what the sin issue, I can use these steps:

1. Confess my sin to God (1 John 1:9)
2. Repent to God and to those I have hurt—meaning I throw my wrongdoing in the "trash" and completely walk away from it toward God's right and good ways (Acts 3:19)
3. Receive God's forgiveness (Ps. 51:7)
4. Try to make restitution for anything I have done wrong (Luke 19:8–9)
5. Submit again to the lordship of Christ and allow His Spirit full access to my life (James 4:7)

Basically, I get rid of everything that is not of God. I allow God to pour His goodness and truth into my life, and I receive all He desires to give me.

Perhaps there are moms who are wracked with guilt over their past failures with their children. Maybe it seems like it is impossible to see anything good come from their past decisions that contributed to pain in their children's lives. We can't go back in time to fix things. We can't turn terrible situations into good. But God can!

I can pray for God's healing for my children spiritually and that He might provide the resources they need. I can trust God to keep His promises to me and to my children, and I can ask Him to create "beauty instead of ashes" (Isa. 61:3). He is an expert at this very thing, thankfully!

I can rest in His sovereignty and let Him carry the weight of other people's problems and their souls—even for my family. I can't carry that weight because it is not mine to carry. If I try to carry the weight of others' heavy burdens, their decisions, their circumstances, or the consequences of their decisions, I will buckle under the load. I am not designed to carry those kinds of burdens, but I can lay them at God's feet and entrust them to Him!

I like to think of myself as one of the friends who carried the paralytic on a mat to Jesus and lowered him down through the roof so Jesus could heal their friend (Mark 2:3–5). I know I can't fix people's hearts or lives. I can't even fix my own. But I know the One who can.

All people answer to God for their own actions. I don't need to try to convict people or be their Holy Spirit. God is perfectly capable of doing that. Honestly, if I try to play Holy Spirit, I will just make people mad at me and repel them from God and myself. I have enough responsibilities on my own plate to take care of. I can seek to bless others. I can pray for them. There are times I may need to confront sin gently, respectfully, and humbly after I have dealt with any sin in my own life (Matt. 7:1–5; 18:15–17). I can help others in healthy ways, but I don't need to try to force their eyes open or make them turn to God. I can set a godly example, love them, and seek to point them to Christ and His healing.

Growing in My Faith Is My Responsibility

Thankfully, if I want to grow in my faith in Christ, no one in this world can stop me. Of course, Satan will not be happy, and he will do what he can to throw me offtrack. He hates it more than anything when a believer begins to truly live by faith and submits to Jesus wholeheartedly. But what peace this truth brings to my heart! If I seriously want to grow in my faith and to know and love my Lord more, God will give me every opportunity to do exactly that. I just want to be sure I take advantage of the instruction, tests, trials, and blessings God provides for me along the way.

I can do many things to feed my faith and help me grow:

- Read the Bible with the focus of wanting to obey anything God asks me to do

- Meditate on and memorize God's promises and His Word
- Stay in the Word and in prayer regularly
- Praise and thank God throughout each day
- Meet with other believers for worship and instruction at a Bible-teaching, Bible-believing church, if at all possible
- Get rid of worldly distractions that would pull me away from God
- Read about the lives of strong believers in Christ who went before me or even who are living now, for inspiration
- Study to be sure I know sound doctrine, always comparing anything any teacher says to the Bible (listening to podcasts of something such as Wayne Grudem's *Systematic Theology* book would be helpful)[2]
- Avoid listening to false teaching
- Pray for and find a godly female mentor, accountability partner, or prayer partner to meet with regularly
- Let my closest friends be people who are very close to God.
- Study the character of God
- Take discipleship classes
- Ask God to take me much deeper
- Welcome the trials and tests that come that will help strengthen my faith
- Journal my prayers and thoughts if that helps me learn
- Notice the things that pull me away from God and remove them from my life, if possible
- Seek God's will for me in everything

If I depend on others to be responsible for my character and my behavior, I will be disappointed. They can't control me or make me do or say anything. My character is an inside job that demonstrates my current relationship with Christ and my level of spiritual maturity. For those of us who like to have control, here is some great news! This is something I get to control—myself, with God's power. When I choose to let God have the control panel in my life, I will have supernatural peace in my mind and heart that defies human explanation.

Extra Responsibility for Young Children

With younger children, I'm responsible for them in certain ways that I'm not responsible for grown adults or even teenagers. They don't have the ability to make their own choices or discern between right and wrong when they are very young. They need their parents' help to make wise choices until they have the ability and capacity to begin to do so for themselves. It is a slow process for children to gradually take on more responsibility and practice making wise choices. They need their parents to mentor and disciple them until they are ready to handle independence.

> "As my children grow up, I transition
> from taking total responsibility . . .
> to releasing them to make more
> and more choices on their own."

As my children grow up, I transition from taking total responsibility for them when they are babies to releasing them to make more and more choices on their own. I will change from having "positional authority" to having "influential authority" because as my children become adults, they will take over their own decision-making responsibilities.

- Positional authority is a position of God-given authority over someone—positions like king, president, CEO, boss, pastor, teacher, husband, or parent. A person in such a position is to be honored, respected, obeyed, and followed as described in the Bible—unless that person asks anyone in their care to sin or condone sin.

- Influential authority is given to those who impact those in positions of authority. An advisor has influential authority over a king. A wife has influential authority over her husband. Think of how Eve and Esther used their influential authority in powerful ways with their husbands, with vastly different outcomes. As our children become adults, we switch over from having a position of authority over them to being more of a trusted advisor.

My children do need to obey me when they are young and still living under my authority (Eph. 6:1–2), but God does not require grown children to obey their parents in the same way that younger children need to. God requires children to always honor their parents (Matt. 15:4–6) even when they are grown. But there is a leaving that happens when children become adults (Gen. 2:24). I am not raising them to keep them for myself. I am raising them so they can learn to fly on wings like eagles and bring great glory to God as grown adults themselves.

As I take responsibility for my own character and behavior, I realize I am not a victim. It is stressful to be a victim, to feel I have no power and that I have to wait on other people to make things right for me. Thankfully, I don't have to complain to God or anyone else. I have choices to make that dramatically impact the quality of my life, and the lives of those around me, no matter what others may do. As I wrestle with denying my sinful nature and I embrace my new identity in Christ and my Spirit-filled life, the gates to deep, lasting peace open wide before me.

A Peaceful Mom's Prayer

Lord,

I know that I alone am responsible for the choices I make and for my obedience to You. I alone am responsible for my sin. I accept this responsibility, and I admit that I have failed so many times. I know that in my own strength, I can't be the woman You call me to be. It is impossible! So I cling to Jesus and His work that was finished on the cross for me two thousand years ago. I invite Your Spirit to have full control in my life to empower me to live the life You desire me to live. I am completely dependent on You, and I receive all of Jesus's power to live in and through me.

Amen.

Finding Victory over My Negative Emotions

There is a way that appears to be right, but in the end it
leads to death. (Proverbs 14:12)

It's clear that God gave us our emotions for our good (even Jesus wept). Our emotions are part of what makes us like God. He has a full range of healthy emotions, too—joy, sadness, grief, anger, jealousy—although, interestingly, one emotion God does not have is fear. He has nothing to be afraid of because He is in control and He is good!

We tend to trust our emotions implicitly. But I think we can all agree that our emotions can also cause us problems and skew our perception of reality, robbing us of God's good gifts. Since we live in a fallen world, our emotions have been affected by sin, too. If we are not careful, we will let them rule over us instead of the other way around. When my negative emotions have a free-for-all in my heart, there is anything but peace. From my perspective at that moment, it seems as if I am seeing correctly and responding correctly. But it is painful for everyone around me and for myself when I am a slave to my emotions.

The fact is no one on earth or in the heavens can take away the peace, love, and joy of Christ from me (Rom. 8:35–39). Those things are mine because they are an ironclad promise from God to all those who belong to Jesus. I have the power to experience all of God's promises as I yield control to Christ alone. This is a key to being a peaceful mom—that I receive the good things God has for me and that I don't let another person, my circumstances, or Satan steal what God has given to me.

Identifying Problem Emotions

Since I have been on this peaceful mom journey for a number of years, I don't get upset nearly as often as I used to—thankfully! But I do still cry at times because I am still human. Sad things happen in life, and it is okay to be sad about them. It is good to feel my emotions at those times. It is not healthy to just stuff them or ignore them. If I do so, I will likely make myself physically ill. Feelings need to be experienced and worked through.

Negative emotions often make us feel as if we're walking in a swirling cloud, or maybe even a raging storm. Before I can deal with the actual problems, I first need to be able to untangle my emotions so that I can see more clearly. Then I can properly identify problem emotions and the issues behind them so I can handle them in healthy ways that honor God, my family, and myself.

Anger is generally a secondary emotion, covering fear or hurt. Sometimes anger can indicate that there may be an issue with pride. Frustration and irritability are magnified by exhaustion, pain, illness, and hormones. Jealousy can be a sign that we are being sinned against, or it may be a sign that we are not thinking biblically. Fear can be a flag that reveals an area where we don't trust the Lord and where our faith may need strengthening. Or fear can signal that we may believe lies from the enemy and that those lies need to be replaced with God's truth.

Until we really dig and ask the Lord to help us examine our deepest beliefs and motives, our tangled emotions can be confusing. God's light brings great clarity and discernment into the darkness as we give Him permission to shine His truth into the deepest parts of our hearts and minds. His Word and Spirit give us the ability to rightly identify what is going on and how we need to address it.

> For the word of God is alive and active. Sharper than any double-edged sword, it penetrates even to dividing soul and spirit, joints and marrow; it judges the thoughts and attitudes of the heart. Nothing in all creation is hidden from God's sight. Everything is uncovered and laid bare before the eyes of him to whom we must give account. (Heb. 4:12–13)

When we're running life's course, it's often difficult to uncover what is really happening. The good news is we don't have to depend completely on our emotions. We don't have to be slaves to our clouded, stormy feelings. Even in the worst of circumstances, God provides ways for us to be peaceful moms. His Word and Spirit provide the light we need to see clearly. If He is in the boat with us, He can calm the raging storm in our hearts and minds.

Let's dig into a few places where we, as women, often get tangled in our emotions, and then let's invite God into the situation.

Righteous Anger Versus Unrighteous Anger

When I am sinned against, that is not okay. If someone is genuinely wronged, this is an appropriate time and place for righteous anger. It is right to hate sin and the pain it causes to the Lord and to people, including myself. I should be angry when I see people being hurt in any way. I should be upset when I see oppression or when I see people suffering. I should want to see things made right and see that justice is served when someone is wronged, including myself. This is righteous anger.

Righteous anger can motivate and empower me to have the courage to seek to change things that are not right, to confront sin in godly ways, and to bring about healing in my family and for those who are mistreated in the world. I can do this in the power of God's Spirit in ways that don't lead to sinful anger. With righteous anger, I can respond in gentleness and with self-control.

If a classmate bullied my son by cursing at him and assaulting him, I would feel righteous anger about the suffering my son endured and the sin committed against him. I would want justice for my child, especially if my child had done nothing to provoke such an attack. I would rightly speak to the principal of the school and possibly even to the police. Righteous anger motivates me to address the sin committed against my son and see that things are made right for him.

> "Righteous anger can motivate
> and empower me to . . .
> confront sin in godly ways."

However, I must be cautious because it is easy to be tempted into unrighteous anger that would be destructive. If I allow my anger to turn into hatred, bitterness, rage, gossip, a desire to hurt someone else, or violence, then I have crossed the line and am responding in a sinful way that dishonors God. I don't get to take vengeance into my own hands. I don't receive a free pass to sin in my motives, thoughts, words, or actions when I am sinned against.

Gentleness is a counterpoint to responding with unrighteous anger. When I demonstrate gentleness, I show that I am in control of myself and that I am acting in love. Rather than responding in a crazy, out-of-control way or in a rage, I can maintain my dignity and poise. I can get my point across to others and my children without abusing them or even being harsh.

I had a problem with screaming and being harsh with my own children when they were younger. I personally taught myself to consciously whisper to them or to sing to them rather than raising my voice. Any time I felt tempted to scream, I forced myself to speak very softly in a nonthreatening way. They responded to gentleness so much more favorably than to my losing control and yelling. Then they could hear my message and not react in fear. I may need to be firm, but I don't want to lose self-control. A mom's anger is scary to her children—and everyone else. As peaceful moms, we are called to act in gentleness.

I also practiced on camera speaking with a friendly, pleasant tone of voice, respectfully asking my children to do things. Yes, I actually did this! I think if I had seen myself on camera losing my temper, I would have been appalled. It helped me to hear my tone of voice objectively and to see my facial expressions when I recorded myself. Then I deleted it quickly!

I would practice saying things like, "Please pick up your toys now. Thanks!" Or, "Time to get your shoes on and grab your backpack. Thank you!" I worked at it until I could make requests in a genuinely pleasant, loving, friendly way with a real smile.

> A gentle answer turns away wrath,
> but a harsh word stirs up anger. (Prov. 15:1)

Sometimes gentleness is more difficult to achieve than other times. But God can give me the power to respond with self-control, even when my children are sinning. That is the time I am most tempted to lose my temper—when they are disobeying or when they are dawdling and making us late. Oh, how I hate being late! In those moments, I need to be even more aware of my tone of voice, asking God to help me demonstrate His gentleness to my children even when I need to be firm.

There are ways I can identify unrighteous versus righteous anger to help me decide how I should handle my anger.

Signs of Unrighteous Anger
- Stems from selfishness, pride, pain, worldly guilt, or fear
- Dishonors God
- Desires to wound other people and make them pay
- Inspires me to tear down others with my own attitudes, actions, words, and behaviors
- Causes me to justify sin in my heart
- Holds on to resentment and bitterness
- Will not forgive
- Takes vengeance for itself
- Results in hatred for people rather than hatred for sin
- Moves me away from God toward Satan

Now that we have seen some signs of anger that displeases God, let's look at some examples.

Examples of Unrighteous Anger
- A mom rightly wants her five-year-old daughter to brush her teeth. When the daughter doesn't brush her teeth, Mom loses her temper.
- A mom may want her children to obey her about finishing up their homework. When it takes longer than she thinks it should for them to finish, Mom loses her temper and raises her voice.
- When her child is not ready for church on time, again, a mom says nothing, but seethes with resentment in her heart.
- When her seven-year-old daughter apologizes for spilling her cereal and milk on the floor, a mom says in exasperation, "What is wrong with you? You are such a klutz!"
- A mom says to her teenage daughter, "I can't believe I had to come pick you up from school just because you threw up. You have ruined my whole day."

- A mom sighs heavily when her child needs help with homework . . . again.

The moms above were angry. Sometimes there were legitimate reasons for the mom to correct her children in the examples above, and sometimes there weren't. I may want to think about whether these kinds of angry mom responses would lead to my children becoming more godly. Would a mom acting in these ways be demonstrating a Christlike example? Do you see the fruit of the Spirit in these illustrations? Love, joy, peace, patience, kindness, goodness, faithfulness, gentleness, and self-control are markedly missing.

Signs of Righteous Anger
- Wants to see relationships restored and reconciled (Matt. 5:9)
- Wants to honor God above all else (1 Cor. 10:31)
- Hates sin like God hates sin (Ps. 11:5)
- Hates to see people hurting (Rom. 13:10)
- Gives the power and boldness of God's Spirit to seek to bring about justice, reconciliation, and healing (2 Cor. 5:18)
- Empowers me to confront wrong and sin (Luke 17:3)
- Forgives quickly and extends grace and mercy to others (Matt. 5:7; 18:21–22)
- Does not hold on to resentment or bitterness (Eph. 4:31)
- Rejoices when true repentance occurs (James 5:19–20)
- Wants good for the other person (Gal. 6:10)
- Wants those who are sinning to turn to Christ (2 Thess. 3:15)
- Loves its enemies (Matt. 5:43–48)
- Leaves vengeance to God (Rom. 12:19)
- Knows that other people are not the real enemy; our enemy is unseen (Eph. 6:12)
- Moves me away from Satan toward God (Eph. 4:26–27)

Thankfully, God wants to help purify my life of things that are toxic to my soul. I don't have to continue on in sin. In Jesus, I can claim victory over sin as His Spirit lives in and through me.

Let's think about some ways we might express righteous anger appropriately toward our children.

Examples of Righteous Anger

- A mom may calmly and sadly say to her daughter, "I am really disappointed to find out that you cheated on your test at school. I expect you to be honest and not to ever cheat. I'm going to talk with your dad about what consequences we need to set up for you, because cheating was wrong. Please hand over all your devices for now and get started on your homework until Dad gets home and we can decide what we need to do as discipline."

- A mom may gently and firmly say to her teenage son, "I am very upset to hear that you have been cursing. In our family, we don't use vulgar words or curse words. This has to stop today. Because you chose to curse, here is the consequence you will experience . . ."

- A mom may softly say to her three-year-old daughter who just lied about using the potty, "I know you don't want to use the potty right now. But it is not okay to lie about it. In our family, we always tell the truth because God wants us to tell the truth. I am upset that you said you went to the potty when you really didn't. Now, please go to the potty for real. And then you will need to [experience an appropriate consequence] because you lied to Mama."

Taming Hormonally Driven Emotions

My family usually caught the brunt of my PMS (premenstrual syndrome) issues. Greg, my husband, was my primary target. Everything seemed to be his fault. The day or two before my period, I usually felt like he needed to change dramatically to be the husband I was sure God wanted him to be. Once my period started, everything was fine again. But my children were also on the receiving end of my out-of-control hormones at times.

I can remember times when my children weren't obeying me. I would reprimand them, but they kept doing whatever it was I told them not to do. I got on them again. And then about the third or fourth time, I sometimes completely lost all semblance of self-control, screaming at them at the top of my lungs.

Even as I was doing this, and even as I saw the look of fear and horror on their faces, I didn't feel like I could stop myself. I felt justified. I felt like I was so right—like what I had to tell them was so important, and they had better change and do what I said no matter what I had to do to make them obey. Afterward, I felt *awful*! That was not the kind of mom I wanted to be! Today as I think back, I don't even know what I was screaming about. I'm so thankful my daughter was too young to remember those incidents. I sure wish I could erase them for the rest of us.

When my hormones are out of whack, I often feel compelled to clean obsessively—and I may decide the rest of my family needs to clean with me. The whole house. Right now. "Let's give away half of our possessions. The house is so cluttered! Ugh! I can't stand it! We live in the biggest pigsty ever. What is wrong with these people—my family—that they make such a mess in my house? Why can't they keep things perfectly clean? Look at the dust! And the toys everywhere. Those toys have to go. And half of our clothes. Yes, right now! This is an emergency. A cleaning emergency. Why can't everyone else see how horrific our living conditions are at this moment except for me?"

Then, invariably, I would be totally fine the next day as soon as my period started. "Oh no! What have I done?" Before I learned about respect and biblical submission, PMS used to throw me, and my whole family, for quite a loop every month. It's hard to accept that your feelings are fairly trustworthy the rest of the month, but suddenly, they are lying to you. I used to always believe the feelings and emotions instead of believing my husband or anyone else. My emotions felt so strong and right. It seemed like the problems I saw were the most urgent problems ever and had to be addressed *right then*! Now that is a flag to me. If my emotions are demanding that I need to take drastic action immediately, I may need to slow down and evaluate things first.

I was amazed that after I had been studying and praying about respect and biblical submission, and when I was submitting myself to Christ and dying to self, I had peace—even in the PMS weeks—most months. In fact, what used to be a big storm each month became a little ripple most of the time, sometimes not even noticeable at all. Thank You, Lord! Now, I just need to get through perimenopause peacefully!

I have learned to catch myself when those awful thoughts start taking my mind captive and to ask Greg if he thinks I might be hormonal. Or I look at the calendar and check to see what day it is in my cycle. If there is a good chance that I am in my PMS time, then I have learned to disregard the messages my emotions are sending to me during that time.

I think of it like I am a pilot flying an airplane during a storm. Normally, I can trust my instrument panel, but during PMS my instrument panel (my feelings) can go haywire. If I follow my feelings, I will probably crash my plane. So, I have learned to think of Greg (or even better, God) as the "control tower," and I allow them to walk me through how to safely land. I do not trust the instrument panel during that time. I think about Scriptures such as this:

> Trust in the LORD with all your heart
> > and lean not on your own understanding;
> > in all your ways submit to him,
> > and he will make your paths straight. (Prov. 3:5–6)

Of course, I need this message *all* the time, not just during PMS! I consciously shift my emotional and spiritual weight from depending on my own understanding, wisdom, and feelings to trusting God's Word.

I also purposely seek to trust my husband's wisdom and his perception of reality rather than my own until I can get my bearings again. (If your husband is not emotionally safe for you to trust, pray about finding a godly woman mentor who may be able to do this instead.)

So, I look to him and ask him to tell me if something with the kids that seems like a big deal really is a big deal or not on those days. If he says it's not a big deal, I trust him and don't trust my feelings—then I wait it out. As my children get older, I get feedback from them as well, especially if Greg is not around. This requires humility, but it spares my family and myself a lot of misery when my out-of-control negative feelings don't rule my heart. If I'm willing and able to ignore my out-of-whack feelings when I am hormonal, I'm being a peaceful mom, for sure!

> "It spares my family and myself a lot of misery when my out-of-control negative feelings don't rule my heart."

I imagine "unplugging" from my emotions for a day or two. When negative feelings start to rise up and tell me I should be angry, disappointed, bitter, or upset with my family, I remind myself, "I can't trust those feelings today. I'm going to wait to think about this later." Or if I feel a compulsion to drastically clean the house, I remind myself to slow down. I remember that super-dramatic changes are stressful for my family, even if I like them at the moment. And I remind myself that a clean house is wonderful, but my relationships with my family are more important.

I write in my prayer journal, like I do every day. I lay my concerns before God. Then I consciously leave it all with Him. I don't carry the emotional weight of the burdens anymore. Jesus carries that weight now, and sometimes my husband helps, too. How freeing to not have to hold on to all that angst!

Something else I have to remember is this: my hormones may be a reason why I am more easily tempted to sin, but they are not an excuse. Sin is still sin even if I am hormonal. I am still accountable to God for my attitudes, motives, thoughts, words, and actions! I need to be aware that this is an area of weakness for me and guard my heart and mind so I can slow down and learn to think rightly.

It is so comforting to me to know that my husband is a rock. I can look to him to find safety in that emotional storm, and I can find shelter in his protective love and care for me. Ultimately, my faith and trust is in Christ to lead me even on the hormonal days. Even if Greg isn't able to support me in the way I think he should on a given day, God will never fail me. I can always depend on Him.

As a pharmacist, I also know there are many ways to try to help treat PMS and peri-menopause medically. You can talk with your doctor or pharmacist about your options, or you can check out a reputable medical website to find medical options and lifestyle changes that may help as well. Having a healthy diet can make a huge difference for many women. I can seek medical help if needed, and most importantly, I can also seek God's help. He can give me the power to override my strong negative feelings and to see with His eyes and His perspective.

CONQUERING NEGATIVE EMOTIONS

Sometimes we may need help with negative emotions. Thankfully, the Lord has provided a number of resources and tools so we don't have to face this challenge alone. He is right there, providing abundantly all we need to have victory over these crazy emotions. He can help us untangle them, identify them, and then handle them in godly ways.

Let's examine a few of the tools the Lord has so generously given us.

Who to Run To

When a Christian is isolated and alone, the enemy has her where he wants her. There is healing, safety, and power in living in community in the body of Christ. We need other believers around us to help us when we stumble. We can turn to others to help us:

- A godly, mentoring wife
- A godly Christian counselor or pastor for more difficult situations
- Our husbands
- Possibly our own mothers or biological sisters, if they know the Lord
- God Himself, most importantly of all

When we choose a person to go to for wise counsel, we want to choose someone who is walking in close relationship with the Lord. Ideally, it may be best to choose a woman for a confidante and prayer partner. However, God can use even an unbelieving husband to help us navigate our negative emotions, if things are not too tense in the marriage and we approach our husband with respect. May God give each of us wisdom about whom we might turn to when we need godly wisdom and advice to help us sort out our negative emotions.

Ultimately, the best source for help is the Lord Himself. There is no one greater, more loving, or wiser than He is. Some of our most powerful tools for victory over negative emotions involve running to Him directly for help.

Prayer

When life's scary circumstances come roaring into my life and into my heart, I have the ability, as a child of God, to decide to trust God with my fears and to continue to rest in His love and peace in my mind. I am not saying this is easy. None of the things I talk about in this book come easily in our own human understanding or strength! They are things we learn as we grow and mature in our faith in Christ. It is a process as we learn to yield to God's wisdom and to allow Him to give us the power we need to do the things we can't do for ourselves.

I know I have personally spent much time wrestling in prayer to decide that I will receive God's peace, His promises, and His rest in spite of uncertainty and in spite of difficult circumstances. I have the power to do this because God's Word is true. His promises are true. He is my fortress, my refuge, my ever-present help in times of trouble (Ps. 46:1).

Because I am a child of God who shares position and inheritance with Christ, I can approach God boldly and with confidence (Heb. 4:16). I like to think about the picture of Jesus in heaven when I pray, as John saw Him in Revelation:

> The hair on his head was white like wool, as white as snow, and his eyes were like blazing fire. His feet were like bronze glowing in a furnace, and his voice was like the sound of rushing waters. In his right hand he held seven stars, and coming out of his mouth was a sharp, double-edged sword. His face was like the sun shining in all its brilliance. (Rev. 1:14–16)

His appearance is so incredibly awesome, holy, and majestic that I know I would be face down before Him in utmost reverence and trembling if I were to see Him. And yet He invites me to approach without fear and to receive His love and all that He has provided for me. I imagine His eyes blazing with the most divine love and His heart that only thinks good thoughts toward me. I can choose to see His perfect character as He reveals Himself to me in the Bible. I can rest on His promises to me to use difficult, painful, or sad things for His good purposes. I know His heart will only act out of the highest wisdom and love on my behalf.

I picture the myriads of angels attending Jesus. I think about His power and sovereignty. Then I imagine leaving my concerns at His feet with confidence that God will do what is best for my child and for me in each situation. I purposely don't mentally pick up that weight of the burden again. When I have an accurate mental picture of who Jesus is and I understand His power and motives toward me, I can truly trust Him.

"It can take some practice to learn to respond in faith rather than fear."

It can take some practice to learn to respond in faith rather than fear. Fortunately, we will have many tests to help us learn this skill. Like when I receive a text that my son's high school is on lockdown (which actually happened as I was working on this chapter!), my first instinct is to be afraid and to imagine all the possible worst-case scenarios. But now, because I know that I don't have to be overcome by fear, I can choose to give God my fear and trust Him, resting in His sovereignty as I pray for my son's protection. When things are particularly difficult, or when I want to connect with God more than ever before, I can also add fasting to my prayers. (For more on the topic of fasting, please check out the post on my *Peaceful Wife* blog, "Ten Reasons to Consider Fasting.")

Jesus possesses all authority in heaven and on earth (Matt. 28:18). He has all power and all wisdom. Who better to take care of my concerns, anger, and sadness? Certainly I can't do better than He can with them. How can I see Him rightly and continue to worry when I see how huge He is and how small my problems and I are?

God gives me other tools, as well, to find victory over my crazy emotions.

Meditation and Praise

I like to meditate on God's promises and His Word. It is His love letter to me. There is always such comfort in Scripture if I am willing to receive God's words as truth. I also love to sing old hymns as well as new praise songs at the top of my voice in the car when I am driving to work or to pick up the kids. Or sometimes I sing when I am cleaning around the house or even at work in the pharmacy before anyone else is there.

I want to keep praises to God and thanksgiving in my heart at all times. That helps keep my heart and mind in the right place. I can't freak out about my circumstances and praise God wholeheartedly at the same time. It is impossible!

I like to go through all the stanzas of many beautiful old hymns because they contain such powerful doctrine. I am greatly encouraged when I meditate on these priceless truths of God. So many of the new praise songs also sweetly remind me to keep my eyes on Christ and to continue to praise Him no matter what troubles I may be experiencing.

In this way, I don't have to be held captive by my initial emotional reaction to trials. I can feel my feelings but I can choose to continue to allow God's Spirit to fill me and to empower me to respond to difficulties in the supernatural power of God with joy and peace (as we will discuss later in chapter 10). I am not peaceful because everything is always sunny and easy. I can be peaceful because God lives in me, loves me, and gives me all of Himself. He gives me the ability to see things and to respond to things in a totally different way than I usually would in my own strength.

I Am Not Responsible for Other People's Emotions

We can't talk about having victory over our own negative emotions without also addressing how we handle other people's negative emotions. So many times, the reason we start down that negative death spiral into terrible emotions is because someone else blasts us with their own negative emotions. Toxic emotions tend to be contagious. I have to consciously remember to separate myself from other people's emotional entanglements or they will gladly drag me right into their negativity.

It's so tempting to think that I need to try to "fix" other people when they have negative emotions. But we are each responsible for our own emotions. I can't control other people. I can only control my own thoughts and emotions with the help of the Spirit of God.

I Am Not Responsible for My Children's Emotions

For some reason, it is especially hard to avoid this compulsion with my own children. After all, I am responsible for them in some ways, and I want to try to fix problems and steer them in the right way in life. But if I attempt to take on total responsibility for their emotions, my children will not learn to take responsibility for their own emotions and will learn to have dysfunctional relationships. My job is to be more of a coach to help them learn to hash through their difficult emotions, rather than to take over and try to do their job for them.

All of us get to be responsible for our own emotions. No one can force someone to be happy. No one can make someone angry. These are things we own for ourselves.

For older teens and grown children, I may just need to give them space when they are having negative emotions unless they are receptive to talking with me or they bring up an issue with me. I can seek to bless them and I can pray for them. I can be there if they want to talk and I can be open to receiving negative feedback if I have wronged them and upset them in some way. Then I can repent, if I need to, in order to bring about reconciliation. Other times, God may prompt me to gently engage verbally with them to lovingly ask about what is really behind the negative emotions and to seek to help them work through things if they are receptive. I can also humbly share things I have learned, if my children are open to my words.

For children who are still under my positional authority, I can seek to guide, nurture, and discipline them if needed. I can instruct my children about how to deal with negative emotions by helping them take their thoughts captive for Christ as we have discussed in chapter 3. I can also help them learn to take their negative feelings to God in prayer and help them learn to claim the promises of God. I can teach them what I am learning myself. They may love to learn to sing praises and thanksgiving to God in the midst of negative feelings, too.

I Shouldn't Measure Myself by Other People's Emotions

Sometimes I may be tempted to try to use other people's emotions as a way to measure how well I am doing spiritually or in my relationship with them. I may think if they are happy, then I am doing a good job, and if they are upset, I must be doing something wrong. Just because my husband or child is upset does not necessarily mean I am in the wrong. Another person's feelings are not always an accurate measurement of how I am doing as a wife and mom.

> "Another person's feelings are not
> always an accurate measurement
> of how I am doing."

I must depend on God's truth, His Word, and His Spirit to help me know how I am doing. I want to listen to other people's feelings and receive feedback graciously, but I must ultimately depend on God's approval more than another person's approval. I want to seek to bless, honor, and respect my husband and children. But if someone else's approval or happiness is more important to me than God's approval and pleasure with me, that is a problem.

MY SON MANIPULATED ME —DANA'S STORY

My relationship with my son has changed just as much as my marriage has from learning from April's journey and applying it! My son has changed so much. The main thing for me was real-izing that I can't control *anyone* else. I really tried to control my elementary school–age son. I tried to make him eat what he didn't want to eat, wear what he didn't want to wear, do what he refused to do. There is obviously a balance, and I definitely don't let him do whatever he wants, but I was being *extreme* with the control.

I would get completely aggravated and frustrated whenever he didn't do exactly what I wanted him to do. I would also put his feelings up in my heart as an idol and the deciding factor of everything. It was like I was living to make sure he didn't get upset. Wow. That was a mistake. He learned to be very manipulative.

My son was *very* rebellious, and it really wasn't until I stopped trying to control him, stopped idolizing him and his behavior, and started focusing on Christ alone to satisfy me, that my son started really changing and being more respectful.

Some ways I catch on to my son now—he'll try to blame me or other people for his "feelings." Now I simply tell him that he is responsible for his own feelings and that no one can "make" him mad. He'll try to manipulate me into doing what he wants, and I simply say, "Your stepdad said X, and that's what the answer is." That was the biggest reinforcement ever!

A Peaceful Mom's Prayer

Lord,

I recognize that I answer to You alone when this life is over. I can't make excuses to You to justify my sin because of my circumstances or the sins of others. I receive this truth that I am responsible for myself emotionally. Help me to live in victory over my negative emotions by the power of Your Spirit.

Amen.

Part Two

Day-to-Day Parenting

Modeling Respect in
All Areas of Life

*Show proper respect to everyone, love the family of believers,
fear God, honor the emperor. (1 Peter 2:17)*

Shortly after a police-shooting incident that rocked our nation, I decided to check in with our twelve-year-old son to make sure he knew how to handle himself with a police officer. I asked him, "So, if a police officer asked you to get out of the middle of the street, what would you do?"

He didn't hesitate, but responded, "Why would I be in the middle of the street?" Well, that was a good question, since we are always careful to walk on the side of the street facing traffic to obey the laws here.

I continued to press a bit. "Okay, but what if you *were* walking in the middle of the street for some reason, and a police officer pulled up in his car and asked you to get out of the middle of the road. What would you do?"

He looked at me like I was crazy and said, as if I should know that the answer was obvious, "I would say, 'Yes, sir,' and go to the side of the road."

RESPECT DEFINED

Respect is such a big word with many different definitions. There is the kind of reverent awe I have for God alone as I stand completely overwhelmed by His majesty, goodness, glory, holiness, and omnipotence. There is the kind of respect I have for people in positions of God-given authority in my life at work, at church, in the government, and in the family. There is the kind of respect that people earn because I see certain character qualities they have—which tends to be the kind of respect our culture primarily emphasizes today. Then there is the kind of respect I have for all people—just because they are created and loved by God. I desire to show common courtesy to everyone because of my own character (God's Spirit living in me), and I want to treat others with dignity, value, and God's love.

The position people hold in my life affects the kind of respect I give them, to a degree. I don't show exactly the same kind of respect to a police officer that I show to my husband. I respect my children in specific but different ways from the way I would respect my boss or my pastor.

God gives people positions of authority to protect, shepherd, provide for, and serve those in their care. They are to make sure that wrong is taken care of and that right wins (Rom. 13:1–7). God's design is to prevent anarchy. Those in authority are to keep people from being harmed and are to make laws, policies, and rules to keep law and order. Leaders are supposed to keep us safe and empower us to live more productive, healthy, peaceful lives. Leaders should be kept accountable by others in positions of authority, so that someone can step in to intervene if leaders abuse their position by harming those in their care. Those with positional authority will answer directly to God for how they handled their positions. The fact is, God created leadership to help create a peaceful society.

And if living in peace isn't good enough motivation, as believers in Christ, God commands us to show proper respect to all the leaders He has provided for us. In fact, Scripture teaches that if we fight against those in positions of God-given leadership over us, we are really fighting God (Rom. 13:1–2). Unless, of course, they ask us to clearly sin or violate God's Word. Then we must choose to "obey God rather than human beings" (Acts 5:29).

Here are some verses about respecting and honoring God-given leadership:

> Let everyone be subject to the governing authorities, for there is no authority except that which God has established. The authorities that exist have been established by God. Consequently, whoever rebels against the authority is rebelling against what God has instituted. . . . For the one in authority is God's servant for your good. . . . Give to everyone what you owe them: If you owe taxes, pay taxes; if revenue, then revenue; if respect, then respect; if honor, then honor. (Rom. 13:1–2, 4, 7)

> Submit yourselves for the Lord's sake to every human authority: whether to the emperor, as the supreme authority, or to governors, who are sent by him to punish those who do wrong and to commend those who do right. For it is God's will that by doing good you should silence the ignorant talk of foolish people. . . . Show proper respect to everyone, love the family of believers, fear God, honor the emperor. (1 Peter 2:13–15, 17)

> Have confidence in your [church] leaders and submit to their authority, because they keep watch over you as those who must give an account. Do this so that their work will be a joy, not a burden, for that would be of no benefit to you. (Heb. 13:17)

Verses about honoring God-given leadership in families and at work can be found in Ephesians 5:22; 6:1; and 6:5–8. (For more on the subject of spiritual authority, please search my blog at www.peacefulwife.com for "spiritual authority.")

RECLAIMING RESPECT

Unfortunately, our culture began to destroy the fabric of our society, since we mostly got rid of the idea of respecting other people decades ago. We also gave up our respect for God and His Word. From there, we trashed the concept of respecting those in positions of God-given authority as well. If God doesn't exist and His Word is not true—as our culture believes—then who cares what He says to do, right? The world views God's design for respecting those in authority as oppressive.

> "When our children see that there is no respect . . . for leaders, they will learn to disrespect those in authority."

Eventually we, as a culture, decided there was no need to respect parents, husbands, teachers, pastors, police officers, government officials, bosses, the elderly, or anyone else. Everyone is fair game to verbally destroy and attack. We have entire television shows that devote themselves to mocking those in positions of God-given authority. Leaders are some of the best fodder for jokes today in popular culture. When our children see that there is no respect anywhere in our culture for leaders, they will learn to disrespect those in authority as well.

Unless parents step in.

DEMONSTRATING REVERENCE AND RESPECT FOR GOD

If I want my kids to genuinely respect others and those in positions of authority, it begins with me reverencing God. I have a healthy fear of Him because I know how powerful, holy, and all-knowing He is. I know that He is the Creator of every person and that each of us is made in His image (Gen. 1:27). I understand that I will have to give an account for every thought, word, and deed in my lifetime to Him (Matt. 12:36; 1 Cor. 4:5).

It's easy sometimes to view God as our "buddy," and we think a lot about His love, grace, forgiveness, and mercy for us in our Christian circles today. Those are very good things, but it is important to remember His holiness, omnipotence, justice, and wrath against sin, too. As I focus on all the character traits of God, I develop a holy fear of Him. I love Him wholeheartedly but also tremble before Him at His might. This helps me remember to show proper reverence for the most powerful Being in the universe who holds my life and my fate in His hands.

Here are some ways I can show respect and honor to God:

- Love the Lord with all my heart, mind, soul, and strength
- Love others with God's love
- Yield fully to Him as Lord and Master in every area of my life—total submission
- Exalt Him far above anyone or anything else in my life
- Praise Him joyfully with spoken or written words
- Sing to Him with all my heart
- Thank Him all throughout the day
- Desire to know Him deeply
- Feast on His Word
- Trust and believe Him
- Be still before Him in anticipation
- Reverence Him for holding all power and reigning in sovereignty over the universe
- Receive God and His Word as truth and life
- Reject every other message and source as false
- Desire to live a holy and obedient life out of gratitude for what Jesus has done for me
- Hate sin the way He does

- Hunger to learn more about His wisdom, Word, and character
- Delight myself in the Lord in good times and in times of suffering
- Approach Him with great humility
- Acknowledge that He is the greatest treasure there is
- Acknowledge that God's wisdom is infinitely greater than any human wisdom
- Trust Him much more than myself
- Seek God's approval alone, not the approval of people or the world
- Ask God to give me His eyes, His heart, and His mind
- Mediate on His Word and memorize it
- Be willing to do anything He asks of me with joy, just because it brings Him pleasure

Part of my respecting God is recognizing His authority in those who are in positions of God-given authority in my life. It's not so much that I respect the particular people themselves or that I agree with them on everything. It's all about my trust in Him to lead me through the channels of leadership He has ordained in my life. God chooses to use those in these positions to bring about His will in my life and in my children's lives. He can even use unbelievers in leadership to accomplish His will (check out the story of Nebuchadnezzar in Jer. 43:10–13 and Dan. 4).

Demonstrating Respect for Those in Authority

God provides human authorities because they are supposed to take care of and bless us. They are supposed to help lead us to accomplish His will in our lives. However, it is important for us to remember that no human, God-given authority usurps God or His Word. God is the ultimate authority. He is the only one worthy of total, unquestioning submission and obedience.

So I must submit with discernment, knowing that ultimately I must obey God above any human. There may be occasions in which I must go against a human authority in a respectful way so that I can honor God's authority. I would want to be sure that what the authority is asking me to do is definitely wrong in God's eyes. I am accountable to God for respecting and honoring those in positions of authority.

> ## "I must submit with discernment, knowing that ultimately I must obey God above any human."

What does that mean? The best way I can teach my children to respect those in authority is by leading them by example:

- Say "Yes, sir" and "Yes, ma'am" if culturally appropriate
- Speak in a calm, polite tone of voice to everyone, but especially to those in positions of authority
- Obey and cooperate with other adults who are in charge in various areas, unless the adult is asking the child to do something that is immoral, illegal, or clearly sinful according to the Bible
- Share concerns or disagreement with those in authority appropriately with proper respect—in private if possible
- Speak respectfully of those in authority even when they are not present
- Pray for God's wisdom and guidance for those in authority over us that His will might be accomplished through them
- Trust that God can and will lead us through those who are in positions of authority over us in most situations
- Encourage others to honor leaders who are not abusing their positions of authority

If I disrespect my children's teacher, my boss, a government official, a police officer, or my husband in front of my children—I am teaching them to disregard authority, and they may pay a steep price for doing so in the future. Sometimes disrespect can cost our children a job, a marriage, or even their lives.

If someone in a position of authority attempts to abuse my children or their leadership position, I want to teach my children to recognize that and to not cooperate with abuse, criminal activity, inappropriate touching, or truly dangerous orders. I want my children to know how to speak up for themselves properly and how to move up the chain of command or find other authorities to report to if someone is wronging them or someone else.

WHEN I WAS PULLED OVER BY A POLICE OFFICER —MY STORY

I saw a new light for a pedestrian walkway downtown. The light was blinking red, and the sign said, "Stop on Red." So I stopped my van and looked. No one was coming. I proceeded as if the blinking red light was a stop sign, and was shocked when a police officer pulled me over. My children were horrified.

I was careful to be very respectful and cooperative with the officer. He was polite and respectful as well. He asked if I knew why he had pulled me over, and I told him I thought I could treat the blinking red light as a stop sign legally. He disagreed and gave me a warning. I was cooperative even though I was confused. When we were driving home, I talked with my children about how this didn't make sense to me and let them know I would check into it. I did, and the police chief decided they had made a mistake in their policy and that I was not in the wrong.

My children were able to witness me treating this officer with respect, even though I didn't believe I had done anything wrong. I never raised my voice. I didn't use any ugly words. This became an opportunity for me to model respect for those in authority.

THE IMPACT OF A MOM'S SPIRITUAL EXAMPLE —LORI'S STORY

My son is sensitive to me worrying or being afraid. It really is true, when all is well and I am peaceful and at rest in Christ—even if things are chaotic on the outside of me—my son is fine. He is at rest. The minute I lose it, he starts freaking out. If I cry, he cries. If I get scared, he gets frightened. What an impact we truly have. It is amazing. When I praise God, my son does, too. When I speak life and truth, so does he!

DEMONSTRATING RESPECT FOR MYSELF

Another way of describing self-respect might be "right thinking about myself" or "thinking that is in line with Scripture." I am not referring to respecting my sinful nature or focusing on my will, my way, my pride, or my selfishness. No, I am in Christ. My old self is dead! I can respect the new life God gives me and seek to be a godly steward of all His gifts to me. I want to receive the truth about what the Bible says about me as a child of God and receive all His gracious promises to me.

What does it mean to respect myself—peaceful mom style?

- I acknowledge that I am made in God's image and have immeasurable worth because God created me and because Jesus loves me and died for me.
- I respect my body by acknowledging that I am fearfully and wonderfully made and being thankful for my body, taking good care of it—not hating or abusing it.
- I respect my sexuality and my body by dressing modestly, not revealing anything that would be inappropriate in public, and enjoying my sexuality in proper context with my husband.

- I respect my life and spiritual, emotional, and physical health by seeking to walk in God's ways and His wisdom, knowing that sin would destroy me on every level.
- I am thankful for the gifts, talents, and abilities God has given me, and I seek to be a good steward of them all.
- I love myself in a godly way, not a selfish way, because I know that God loves me. I receive God's love for me gladly.
- My life is all about God, not about self.
- I can receive the love of other people, including my husband and children.
- I am able to share my perspective, feelings, and needs appropriately without exalting self and without pride.
- I receive that God's Word and His promises apply to me, too, not just to others.
- I take good care of my body, mind, soul, nutritional needs, and health. I seek to do what is best for myself in all these areas.
- I have healthy boundaries emotionally and spiritually and am able to say no when this would please the Lord.
- I take responsibility for my own spiritual growth and my own emotions.
- I do not take on responsibilities that belong to others and to God.
- I do not abuse myself spiritually, mentally, verbally, emotionally, or physically, and I seek not to sin against myself.
- I know when I need to remove myself from a very toxic situation, if I am being truly abused.
- I seek God's wisdom about how to live my life, and I seek to avoid foolish decisions.
- I am careful not to put myself in tempting situations. I guard my heart.
- I am careful not to have any addictions to anything except for Jesus.
- I have a healthy understanding of who I am versus who God is.
- I seek to avoid debt and manage my finances well, acknowledging

that all I have comes from God and I am accountable to Him for how I handle it.

- I am able to stand up for myself against sin if necessary while still being respectful of others.
- I don't allow anyone or anything to steal the treasures I have in Christ.
- I honor and cherish God's design of femininity for me.

I acknowledge that I—primarily—set the emotional temperature for my marriage, family, and home as the wife and mom. I know I need to take good care of myself so I can take good care of everyone else.

Once I learn to think rightly about God and about myself, I am ready to focus on how I relate to others, including my family members. It is tempting to think that I can treat my family much worse than I treat strangers or acquaintances. Consciously or subconsciously, I might think, "These people have to love me, so I don't have to watch my attitude or approach with them. I can 'be myself' around my family." What I really mean if I think that way is that I want freedom to be my sinful self around them. No, not at all! I am free to be my new self in Christ.

When I understand God's heart, I know that He counts the way I treat other people, including my family, as a measure of my love for Him (Matt. 25:31–46). God declares that I cannot love Him and hate a person whom He created and loves (1 John 4:20). A test of my love for God is that I treat the other people He created and loves with honor and respect. I also realize that the way I treat my family can richly bless them or immeasurably harm them. I want to use my influence to build up my loved ones, not to tear them down.

Demonstrating Respect to My Children's Father

Something that shocked me as I focused on becoming a godly, respectful wife was how much my children began to change. God exposed the pride, self-righteousness, disrespect, and control in my heart to which I had been blind for over fourteen years. He showed me that I had not been setting a good example of godly femininity and biblical marriage. I apologized and repented to my husband in December 2008, and I apologized and repented to our children. Our son was seven, and our daughter was two at the time. Immediately, as I began to seek to speak respectfully and act respectfully to Greg, our children began to imitate my new tone and attitude.

Eventually, Greg began to feel safe enough to start trying to be more involved with the children, once he realized I wasn't going to constantly criticize him or complain about how he did things differently from my way. And then, slowly, he began to back me up, too.

> "When everyone treats everyone
> else with respect in the family,
> there is sweet peace.

For the first time, we began to have a united front with our children. If one parent said something, the other parent would also uphold that decision. We had each other's backs. We didn't always agree, of course, so then we would speak privately and respectfully with each other about how to handle various situations. I honored his leadership if we couldn't come to a consensus. Then, in front of the children, we showed unity. They began to obey more readily and to show much more respect for both of us. I began to experience a lot more peace as a mom through this experience. When everyone treats everyone else with respect in the family, there is sweet peace and greater harmony for us all.

Here are some ways I can do my part in presenting a united front to our children:

- Speak with a respectful, pleasant tone of voice to their dad
- Avoid undermining his authority, criticizing him, or arguing with him in front of them

- Uphold Dad's decisions and rules, even when he is gone, even if I don't agree with them
- Share my concerns calmly with him
- Approach Dad with godly humility and be open to seek to understand his perspective and wisdom
- Have major discussions in private whenever possible
- Speak highly—in a truthful way, not a tall-tale, flattering way—of Dad even when he is not around
- Approach him with suggestions and requests rather than directives or demands
- Stop and give all my attention to Dad when he is speaking, and encourage the children to do the same whenever possible
- Teach my children how to speak to their father and about their father in ways that honor him
- Help the children learn to appreciate Daddy's special ways of showing love that are different from Mom's

Of course, ideally, Dad would also uphold Mom's decisions and would not disrespect Mom in front of the children, either. For more about how to respect your husband in a God-honoring way, please refer to my first book, *The Peaceful Wife: Living in Submission to Christ as Lord.*

Note: This section is speaking about situations in which a dad is not asking his wife or children to sin. If a man is trying to lead his family into obvious sin, a mom may have to confront the dad in a humble, respectful way and would not be able to follow him or lead their children into clear sin. If there are serious issues going on in a marriage or with the children (abuse, uncontrolled mental health issues, major unrepentant sin, drug or alcohol addictions, severe spiritual oppression), please seek appropriate counsel. This book is not designed to be a resource for those specific situations. God's Word always applies. But those in extreme situations may need additional resources and specific counsel that I am not able to provide here. Moms, we are accountable to God—and often to the government—to not knowingly allow our children to be abused.

Demonstrating Respect for My Husband

I cover this topic in much greater detail in my first book, but here is a recap of some of the best ways I can show genuine honor and respect to my husband as I seek to model honoring him as a man and as the head of my home. Many of these suggestions would also be appropriate ways to approach a father in a co-parenting situation. Please keep in mind that each husband may have his own preferences, and different cultures vary in what is considered to be respectful as well. Respect is not always one size fits all.

I can honor and respect my husband in these ways:

- Let him make his own decisions about what he eats, what he wears, and so forth
- Let him decide how he wants to spend his time
- Trust him to handle his relationships with his friends and family
- Avoid giving unsolicited advice
- Approach him with good manners, a friendly tone of voice, and a smile when I ask him to do something or need help
- Share my concerns, desires, and ideas humbly, gently, and calmly
- Be a real friend and a safe place for him to come home to
- Seek to be calm and flexible when things start to go wrong
- Smile at him genuinely just to bless him
- Use a friendly tone of voice whenever possible
- Treat him like an equal adult, not like a child
- Thank him for the things he does for the family
- Avoid being contentious
- Approach him with humility, knowing that God has given him wisdom to share, too
- Seek to understand his very different masculine perspective

- Assume the best whenever possible, rather than the worst
- Don't look down on him with a critical spirit
- Don't assume his sin is worse than my sin
- Don't argue or complain
- Receive his compliments, help, and gifts cheerfully and joyfully
- Accept him for who he is without trying to change him
- Enjoy and appreciate him
- Be peaceful and joyful in Christ
- Be content and thankful in everything
- Respond with grace, dignity, and poise even if he doesn't do what I would like

As I treat my husband (or my children's father, even if he is not my husband) with genuine respect, my children witness how godly, peaceful moms treat other people. They see the premise that we treat others well because we love Jesus. They begin to understand that all people have inherent worth in Christ, including them.

Demonstrating Respect for My Children

While my children need to see me treating other adults and those in authority with proper respect, they also will imitate the way I speak to them and how I treat them as they decide how to treat their siblings and friends. I noticed that if I use a harsh tone with one of my children about something, that child tends to use the same harsh tone and words with a sibling later. I want to set a healthy example for them to follow. When I treat my children with respect, I am not exasperating them (Eph. 6:4), so they will be much more peaceful, which lets me also enjoy greater peace. Everyone wins!

These are some ways that I can show respect to my children:

- Generally use a respectful, pleasant tone of voice (unless there is an emergency and I need to yell to keep them from danger)

- Use a respectful, firm tone of voice if they are in trouble
- Sometimes do things with them that they love to do
- Listen to them and seek to understand their perspectives
- Show them their feelings are important to me
- Control my temper and exhibit patience, gentleness, and self-control
- As they get older, ask for their permission before sharing stories about them
- Use caution in what I share on social media
- Be cautious about making promises, but always try to keep my promises if I do make them
- Be a safe place for them to share their struggles
- Allow them to have their God-given free will and not try to control their thoughts
- Talk through consequences ahead of time whenever possible and set appropriate consequences for sinful or wrong behavior
- Be consistent with discipline so they know what to expect
- Talk through spiritual issues with them honestly and authentically
- Give them age-appropriate responsibilities
- Let them make their own decisions more and more as they mature and as they show that they are trustworthy
- Teach them God's ways and His wisdom
- Pray with them and for them in a humble, loving, compassionate way
- Be honest with them
- Be trustworthy and responsible as a parent
- Teach them their worth in Christ
- Teach them to be godly stewards of the gifts God has given them as I demonstrate these things in my own life
- Seek to do what is truly best for them in God's eyes and in the light of eternity
- Be sure my words speak God's life into their hearts

- Set the tone for a loving, warm, peaceful, joyful, safe home
- Be welcoming
- Accept who my children are and celebrate their unique personalities
- Nourish and nurture their souls, bodies, and minds with good, healthy things
- Protect them from harm whenever it is possible—although I need to be careful to do this in a balanced way and not to be overly protective or irresponsible
- Discipline a child privately when possible, away from siblings or friends if the issue doesn't involve the other children
- Stay as close to God as possible and be filled up with His Spirit so that I have the wisdom, discernment, and power I need to respond to my children in God's ways, not in my own flesh

RESPECTING MY HUSBAND IN TOUGH DECISIONS —JOANNE'S STORY

Six months ago, God brought me to my knees over my disrespect of my non-Christian husband of twenty-two years. Since then, I've been trying to respect him. I have two older teens, who both know and love the Lord. Last weekend, my daughter and her Christian boyfriend attended a party together that finished at midnight. She got home an hour and a half later (it was a twenty-minute drive away). She said they had been to the drive-through at McDonalds. She hates fast food.

I was in knots. Not only because, as a mother, I was up worrying if they were safe, but also because I was so afraid they had been "up to something." In the morning, I asked my husband what I should say to my daughter regarding her late night. He said, "Don't say anything." Okay, that was *not* what I wanted to hear! I needed to challenge her, ask her what she was up to, voice my fears and suspicions, and generally thrash out whether she was guarding herself!

I decided to honor my husband's leadership. I was glad to because I'd been asking the Lord to show me ways to respect my husband, and I have been telling God that I trust Him to lead me and our family through my non-Christian husband. So this was a chance to prove I meant what I had prayed. But I didn't agree with him—or like his decision! I was preoccupied with worries to the point that I couldn't sleep, but was convicted not to say anything to her for three days.

Finally, after getting up extremely early to pray this morning, I had a very small, simple text discussion with my daughter, which basically told me I had *nothing* to worry about! Now I see that had I gone ahead in disobedience and made a massive "discussion" on Sunday, I would have made everything so much worse and caused unnecessary angst.

It is a difficult balance—parenting teens. To be too heavy-handed just sends them the other way. But they do need to be accountable to their parents and know that some things are unacceptable. I am so grateful to God for His grace to me in this area, and for my precious, wise husband who guides me (when I let him) and reins in my hotheaded approach.

MY SON COULD SEE THAT I WAS IN CHARGE, NOT DADDY —SHANNON'S STORY
(SHANNON POPKIN, AUTHOR OF *CONTROL GIRL*)

When my son was about three, I was out grocery shopping when I got a call from him on my husband's phone. "Mommy?" he said in his sweet, raspy voice. "Can I go spwash in Jaden's pool?" It was a kiddie pool in our neighbor's driveway.

"Did you ask Daddy?" I asked.

"Daddy said yes," he said, "but I told him we hadda call you, 'cause you are da controller of us. Right, Mom?"

I was so mortified. The controller of my kids? The one their dad should call if they needed permission? How had my son gotten *that* impression?

But if I'm honest, I know how. I suppose it happened in a thousand small, subtle ways, spaced out over days and weeks and years. I never would have blatantly *said*, "I'm the boss of our family. I'm in control." But I did give lots of little hints. Like scolding Ken for using the wrong bowls. Or overruling on the TV shows he said the kids could watch. Or rolling my eyes when he put the toddler's jacket on the baby.

Without meaning to, I regularly communicated that I outranked Daddy: that he answered to me—the expert. And since I'd made it infinitely clear that Daddy couldn't be trusted when I *was* home, no wonder my son doubted if he could be trusted when I wasn't.

It's interesting that my son saw me as a "Control Girl," because back then I just *didn't*. I figured that since I was the primary caregiver, it was natural for me to take charge. Having been with the kids for the past 642 hours in a row, I knew exactly which sippy cup went to which kid, which direction the grilled cheese sandwiches must be cut, and which whimpers from the crib could be ignored rather than acted upon.

Mommy knew these things. Daddy didn't. I mean, you could *ask* Daddy, but if you wanted a definitive answer, you should ask Mom. This was the message my kids had gotten loud and clear in our household.

But there's something I recognize now, which I didn't as a young mom. Kids need their daddy to be their leader. This creates security and trust and sets a foundation for the home. Kids also need to see their mom *respecting* their dad as the leader and treating him as such. And they need this far more desperately than they need the correct sippy cup or age-appropriate TV shows.

Now, it can be tricky, especially if Daddy is coming and going. And I'm not saying that a wife shouldn't remind her husband to cut the hot dog in tiny pieces for their one-year-old. But when she sighs and snatches the plate from his hand to cut it herself, she's chopping away—little by little—at more than a hot dog. She's undercutting the leadership God intended her husband to have. And none of this is lost on that pair of eyes, looking up at both parents.

That phone call about the kiddie pool was a wake-up call for me. I want my children to respect their daddy and see him as the leader. But this starts with me. Rather than sighing or rolling my eyes or snatching control from my husband, I need to invite my husband to lead. This involves treating him like a leader and responding to him the way I would any other leader—with respect and honor. When my kids see their mom treating their dad as the leader, they are invited to do the same.

MY LIFE FEELS OUT OF CONTROL, SO I'LL TRY TO CONTROL MY KIDS —EMMA'S STORY

I was in the middle of my life. I had two tweens two years apart. My husband had become a workaholic, and I was responsible for everything at home, even the yard work. I couldn't even get my husband to take out the garbage. On top of it, I worked full time.

I resented all this responsibility. I loved being a mom, but I really wanted my husband to be my partner in all of this. I wanted to be a perfect wife, a perfect mom, a perfect employee, daughter, and friend. In order for that to happen, I had to run a tight ship. Time was always ticking, and I operated like a drill sergeant. At some point, I developed what I call "kick the dog" syndrome because I was irritated by other things: work, time rush, or mostly my husband's stonewalling, disconnection, and criticism.

I wanted to control something. So I controlled my kids. They needed to hurry up, be quiet, do what I said, no questions asked. I was already irritated about my life. I didn't need to have more pushback from my kids. Besides, I am the parent, and they are the kids, right? They are supposed to obey their parents. I became a scary person to my kids. I would yell at them, belittle them, and even be aggressive, although not abusive. I would try to force conversations, and I would escalate arguments.

At one point, my son had to pick out some colored paper for a school project, and he was so scared he was going to choose a color of paper I would not approve of that he broke down in the store and refused to choose. He just wanted me to do it so that he wouldn't get in trouble. My daughter was shutting down emotionally, too. She would not talk to me about her day and was just very cold and withdrawn. One time she told me that she doesn't want to talk to me because I always "freak out."

I knew I was losing my kids. I had lost my husband somehow, and now I was losing them, too. How could I be to the point that I was losing all the people that meant the most to me? In desperation, I began to search for a solution to my problem in my marriage and came to know Christ as both Savior and Lord after reading www.peacefulwife.com. It was a powerful experience to have such a great awakening. I asked God for forgiveness. I asked my husband and kids for forgiveness. I was invigorated to make it up to everyone I had hurt.

I started to see my kids as individuals and not just "kids." I started to share my faith with them. My son started to find his voice the more I respected him as a male. Yes, he was still a child, but just respecting him as a person of his own, a child of God, went a long way.

I also learned about just listening to my daughter—how she felt and her emotions. Not trying to "fix" them or control the situation or run in and solve all her problems. Through all of this, I realized I had three big sins I needed to be on guard about at all times: control, perfectionism, and pride. Especially perfectionism.

As God helped me see my sin and how my motives were locked in pride, I began to let go of the need to have things my way. I would experiment a bit with this and was so surprised at how things turned out better and with fewer problems when I would stop trying to control things. I had to learn a balance, though. I would swing wildly between control and total indifference as I learned to find a good spot in the middle. But by listening to God and the Holy Spirit inside me, I found God's "narrow path" more quickly.

Today, although the relationship with my husband is still not where I would like it to be, I have my kids back. I have been able to watch my son grow in confidence and courage. He is not cowering in fear anymore. He feels like an important part of the family and knows his voice is heard. I am so proud of him, and I find that he is funny, charming, sensitive, and loving.

I have been able to gain a closeness with my daughter that I never could have dreamed of. She opens up to me, and I feel privileged to see a glimpse of her life. She is starting to let go of her own perfectionism as she sees me model that, too. She is not so under pressure to perform and succeed. I have found a new love of my children that I never knew before. They feel safer with me, more open and connected.

Learning respect was a turning point in my life. I know that I have become a much better person through these trials and although they were painful for the time, in the long run, I have far less pain and sadness in my life than I did before. I will always keep God as first in my life and seek Him to learn all the days of my life.

A Peaceful Mom's Prayer

Lord,

My children are watching me so very attentively every moment. Change my mind and heart. Make me more like Jesus by Your power. I can't model respect properly or do anything good on my own in my flesh. But my old flesh is dead now, and I am alive in Jesus. Empower me to set the godly example You desire me to set as I seek to honor and respect those around me, especially my husband and those in positions of God-given authority. Empower me to demonstrate genuine respect as I interact with my children as well, that You might be greatly glorified!

Amen.

Loving My Children "Too Much"

*Anyone who loves their son or daughter more than me is not
worthy of me. (Matthew 10:37)*

Years ago, I became obsessed with the idea of having a baby. It was time for us to have children—in my mind—and nothing was going to stop me. I had waited six years already for Greg to have a job with insurance benefits, and he finally had it! I knew I wanted to be able to work part time once I had children. So as soon as the insurance thing was out of the way, there was no time to waste!

I didn't really stop to ask Greg what he wanted or about his concerns. I assumed there was no way this couldn't be God's will. The only thing I could see was my goal—motherhood. I pressured and forced my way into motherhood rather than allowing Greg to have a voice and to be part of the process, too. If he had any hesitation, he was obviously "fighting God's will." A stage of life that could have been a joyous time of unity was marred because of my approach.

Once our first baby was born, my life revolved so much around him that Greg felt very left out, I found out later. I was nursing, so Greg couldn't really help with feedings. But I was also "the expert parent."

After all, I was the one who read all the baby-care websites and articles. I knew the latest medical advice. I took over everything that had to do with taking care of our baby, most of the time, because I could do it "better" than Greg could. It was all up to me, and things had to be exactly right—my way.

My child had become my idol—the driving force behind what I did.

AM I WILLING TO SACRIFICE ANYTHING FOR GOD?

God calls us to love Him with all our hearts, souls, minds, and strength. That is the Greatest Commandment according to Christ (Matt. 22:36–37). He also says something very radical about the cost of being a follower of His—that we must be willing to put Him far above anyone and anything else in our lives, that we must "hate" our own families, or we can't be His disciples (Luke 14:26).

That doesn't sound right, does it? After all, the second greatest commandment Jesus gave us was to *love* all other people as we love ourselves (Matt. 22:39). So how can He tell us that we must hate those who are dearest to us and even hate our own lives? Of course, God's Word also commands us in multiple places not to hate anyone else. So it is clear that Jesus doesn't literally mean we are to hate our families and our own lives in the sense that we don't value them, we don't love them, we don't want to be with them, we mistreat them, and we wish bad things on them. So what could He mean?

Sacrificing the Unthinkable

One of the most powerful stories in the Bible, in my view, is the story of Abraham. God loved Abraham, chose him from all the men on earth and made a covenant with him that He would bless him and make him into a great nation (Gen. 12:1–3). He chose Abraham's future children as His special people. God said to Abraham (who was still called Abram at that point in his life), "Do not be afraid, Abram. I am your shield, your very great reward" (Gen. 15:1). He commanded Abraham to leave his family and go to a new land, the land God would give to Abraham and his many descendants. He made an everlasting covenant to bless Abraham and his offspring, even though Abraham and Sarah were childless.

God promised Abraham and his wife, Sarah, a son when Abraham was seventy-five years old, but that baby did not come until Abraham was one hundred and Sarah was ninety. Isaac was born to this over-joyed couple, and he was the most precious gift either of them could have imagined. But when Isaac was older, God appeared to Abraham again: "Take your son, your only son, whom you love—Isaac—and go to the region of Moriah. Sacrifice him there as a burnt offering on a mountain I will show you" (Gen. 22:2).

> ## "[Abraham] did not hold anything back from God, not even the son he loved so dearly."

What a confusing command to receive from God after God had finally given Abraham and Sarah this precious child. How could He ask such a thing? Abraham took Isaac the next morning to Mount Moriah (which, interestingly, is the same mountain where God instructed Solomon to build His temple in Jerusalem in about 832 BC). Abraham demonstrated total faith and acted in complete obedience to what God asked him to do. He did not hold anything back from God, not even the son he loved so dearly.

It wasn't that Abraham hated Isaac. He loved Isaac dearly! But he loved God supremely and trusted God no matter what He asked him to do. He knew that God could raise Isaac from the dead if necessary and trusted God's promise that Isaac would carry on his line as God had said. It was not until Abraham had already bound Isaac, laid him on the altar, and raised a knife to kill his son that an angel stopped him and God provided a ram that was stuck in the thicket to be a replacement sacrifice for Isaac. God spoke to Abraham: "'Do not lay a hand on the boy,' he said. 'Do not do anything to him. Now I know that you fear God, because you have not withheld from me your son, your only son'" (Gen. 22:12).

God richly blessed Abraham because he trusted God completely and did not hesitate to give his son to Him. There are special blessings and treasures that God reserves only for those who completely yield everything to Him.

> The angel of the LORD called to Abraham from heaven a second time and said, "I swear by myself, declares the LORD, that because you have done this and have not withheld your son, your only son, I will surely bless you and make your descendants as numerous as the stars in the sky and as the sand on the seashore. Your descendants will take possession of the cities of their enemies, and through your offspring all nations on earth will be blessed, because you have obeyed me." (Gen. 22:15–18)

How incredible to see that not only was Abraham blessed by God because of his total surrender and obedience, but all his descendants were blessed through his obedience in very specific ways. And all the nations of the earth would be blessed because God would send Jesus through Abraham's descendants. If Abraham had refused to obey God, his story and history would have been so very different. God would have still sent His Messiah, but surely He would have chosen someone else to be Jesus's ancestor.

Amazingly, hundreds and hundreds of years later, God would offer His only Son, Jesus, as a sacrifice for us in that same city within view of the same mountain. But when God offered His Son, there was no substitute. He went through with His offering because He knew it was the only way for us to be able to come to Him. What God asked Abraham to be willing to do—maybe as much as two thousand years earlier—God

Himself did for us. God gave up everything that was dear to Him for us, including the life of His only Son. Now He gives us the opportunity to give up everything for Him.

For me to follow Christ as Lord, I must be willing to lay down all that I have and all that I love on the altar before Him. I hold nothing back. He is now my Lord. He is the Master. I trust everything in my life and all that is most precious to me into His loving, sovereign hands. I say with Jesus in the garden of Gethsemane, "Not my will, but yours be done" (Luke 22:42).

God asks the same thing of me that He asked of Abraham. He wants to see that I love Him more than anyone or anything else in this world. He asks me to lay my husband, my children, my health, my future, and all that I have on a figurative altar before Him—not knowing what He may do with any of it. But what I do know is that God's heart and His intentions are always good. This is how I show God that I love and trust Him wholeheartedly—I am willing to give up what is most precious to me.

It is not that I literally hate my family and loved ones. I love them with God's love! But if one were to compare my love for Christ and my love for my family, my love for my Lord is to be so much higher and greater than my love for my husband and children—or any other person—that my love for people would practically look like hatred compared to my love for God. It may seem counterintuitive at first, but when my love for God is so much greater than my love for my children, this is a path to great peace. I am no longer grasping and desperate for anything. My contentment is in Christ, so my tranquility is supernatural and unshakable.

Sometimes God's plans may involve Him asking us to do things that are unimaginable. It is possible that He may ask me to release my children into struggles at school, a serious illness, or even death. I don't want to face a challenge like that. But if I do, I want to have things resolved in my mind in advance about how I want to handle this. How

I long to follow the precious examples of Abraham and believers like George Mueller.

Facing a Child's Imminent Death

George Mueller was a Christian who lived in the 1800s in England. He had incredible faith in the Lord and, arguably, one of the most powerful prayer lives in Christian history. He felt led by God to start an orphanage in 1835, primarily to show other believers how faithfully God provides for His people who trust Him and pray in faith. Mueller eventually cared for over ten thousand orphans over his lifetime and handled over $8 million, but he never asked people for any money. He never publicized the needs of the children. He simply prayed with his wife and staff, and God brought about the funding, supplies, and resources that were needed. Sometimes there were severe tests, but God always provided, and the children always had food, clothing, and shelter.

Mueller writes,

> In July, 1853, it pleased the Lord to try my faith in a way in which before it had not been tried. My beloved daughter and only child . . . was taken ill on June 20th. . . . On July 3rd there seemed no hope of her recovery. Now was the trial of faith. But faith triumphed. My beloved wife and I were enabled to give her up into the hands of the Lord. He sustained us both exceedingly. . . . Though my only and beloved child was brought near the grave, yet was my soul in perfect peace, satisfied with the will of my Heavenly Father, being assured that He would only do that for her and her parents, which in the end would be the best. . . . The Father in Heaven said, as it were, by this His dispensation "Art thou willing to give up this child to me?" My heart responded, As it seems good to Thee, my Heavenly Father. Thy will be done.[3]

Mueller's daughter eventually recovered, which was quite a miracle, but Mueller and his wife were prepared to release her to God, knowing He would do what was ultimately best for them and for His glory. Mueller was emphatic that the great faith he exercised was totally available to every believer in Christ. He showed this same faith when the Lord called his beloved wife home years later. His peace was unwavering.

When my trust is 100 percent in the Lord, His goodness, and sovereignty, I can face even the most difficult trials with the supernatural peace of God flooding my soul. If I truly believe He knows best and I rest in His promises, I can entrust Him with sickness, hardships, suffering, and even death.

I have a number of friends who have had to face this very thing, losing their sweet young children to a miscarriage, an illness, or an accident. But my friends who truly know Christ cling to Him. He becomes more precious than ever, even in those times of darkest grief. Their pain and sadness is intense, but they are not without hope. Many times, God later uses those who have been through such tragedies to greatly bless others by their testimonies of faith. He may even use these tragedies to lead many into the kingdom of Christ.

He is with me even in "the darkest valley" so that I will "fear no evil" (Ps. 23:4). He can and will comfort me if He decides it is best to take me through such a dark place. I will not be alone. How I long to experience the blessing that comes from my obedience and to see how God may use my obedience to Him to bless my family, generations to come, and maybe . . . other people all over the world! Just like He used Abraham and George Mueller.

How Can I Tell if I Idolize My Children?

Most of us balk at the idea that our children may be an idol, but it's easy to fall into allowing our status as parents to define us. Our culture applauds those who center their lives around their children, so this has become pretty normal today. We may not even realize we are idolizing our children. An idol is anything in my life that takes precedence over God and His plans. But it is sometimes difficult to identify when we've pushed God off the throne.

Fear is often a signal that I may be dealing with idolatry.

For me, fear is often a signal that whatever is the opposite of my fear is something I am cherishing more than Christ in my heart. When I see a lot of fear, I know I need to lay that issue before God on the altar in my mind and leave it with Him. I also need to check my heart for unbelief in God and ask God to help increase my faith. I have to personally get to the place (sometimes after much wrestling) where I can genuinely lay down every single person and issue in my life except Jesus and be willing to be content with Him alone, whether I had any of the rest of the things I wanted or not.

Before we examine the ways that we sometimes idolize our children, let's examine some signs of idolatry:

- I have great fear at the thought of not having my idol.
- If someone tries to take away my idol, I will fight that person or give in to despair.
- Thoughts about this thing consume me. I believe I have to have this thing, idea, or relationship, or I can't be content in life.
- The thing I want so desperately is not Jesus.
- I might be willing to try to use Jesus to get my idol, but then I am devastated when He doesn't give me what I really want, which is my idol, not Him.
- I have a lot of anxiety, depression, loneliness, frustration, and bitterness because I don't have the thing I want the most in my life.
- I may feel bitter toward God for withholding my greatest desire from me.

- My faith is primarily in myself or the things I desire, not in Christ.
- I am willing to make great sacrifices—time, large amounts of money, relationships, to name a few—to have my idol.
- This is the primary thing on my heart and mind most of the time.
- My idol is the thing I look to for security, purpose, and meaning in my life.

Here are some things I might say to myself, or possibly out loud to others, if I put a desire for having a baby above Christ in my heart:

- I have to have a baby! If I don't have a baby, life is not worth living.
- If my husband won't have children with me, I'll find someone who will give me the children I want.
- If I can't have a family, God has wronged me and I can't trust Him.
- If I am not needed as a mom, I am worthless as a woman.
- Children are my whole life! They are my only purpose!
- If I can't have another child (or a certain number of children), I will never be content.
- I would do *anything* to have a child!
- Once my children are gone, I'll have nothing.

There are other ways I can set my children above God in my heart and make them into idols as well. This list is more about things I may do once my children are in my life:

- I expect them to meet the deepest spiritual and emotional needs of my soul that only Jesus can meet.
- I try to make them responsible for my happiness instead of being responsible for my own emotions and spiritual well-being.
- I try to live vicariously through them and base my worth on what they do and the praise they receive.

- I center my life around my children as if they are the focal point of my universe.
- I exalt my children's happiness so that it is never acceptable for them to be upset, to cry, or to have difficulty of any kind.
- I make their approval the most important thing.
- I make their safety the most important thing to the point that I am overprotective and even damaging to their development and independence.
- I allow my fears about things that could go wrong with my children to become all-consuming.
- I become obsessed with trying to keep my children from ever being sick.
- I expect them to be perfect little robot servants who always do exactly what I want them to do, and I become exasperated when they reveal their sinful nature and imperfections.

Is It Really Harmful to Idolize My Children?

When I idolize my children, I set my desires for them on the throne of my heart. I trust what I want for them to bring me the greatest fulfillment in life. I am not trusting God. Really, I am trusting self. Idolatry always leads to self-harm in some way or another, not peace for myself. At first, I will hurt myself because of my high anxiety levels as I try to make my idol bring contentment that it can't possibly give to me. Idolatry can only lead to disappointment, dissatisfaction, frustration, depression, and fear. I am sabotaging the very things I want most in my relationship with my children when I idolize them. That is a miserable, stressful way to live.

I also hurt my fellowship with God because God will not allow me to have full fellowship with Him when I am putting some other person, thing, or desire above Him in my life. He counts my idolatry against Him as if it is adultery in a marriage covenant. This greatly offends Him, understandably. He is worthy of being on the throne, and nothing else deserves to be there. When I put my children on the throne of my life and put my faith and hope in them and my desires for them, I forsake my faith and trust in God. Without faith in God, it is impossible to please Him (Heb. 11:6).

Unfortunately, not only do I hurt myself and my fellowship with God when I make my children into idols, but I also hurt my children. This makes it really tough for them to experience a peaceful family life. When I expect my children (or any person) to meet needs that only God can meet in my life, when I expect perfection, or I demand that they do certain things to make me happy, I put an incredible amount of pressure on them. I can't lay my own responsibilities for my emotional and spiritual well-being on their shoulders. For one person to carry that kind of weight for another is soul crushing. Only Jesus can carry that kind of weight for me.

Idolatry of my children destroys them, my relationship with them, and me.

No human can make anyone else happy or spiritually fill up another person. A child in such a situation learns that he is supposed to have unhealthy, dysfunctional boundaries, and that he is responsible for other people's emotions that he really can't control. If he tries to control things that he doesn't have power over, he will be stressed, anxious, and frustrated. He learns to be enmeshed or codependent, and these things often carry through into his relationships as an adult—especially into his marriage and his own parenting.

He learns that it is normal for a woman he loves to try to control him and for him to try to take on responsibility for her happiness. He learns to be a people pleaser. Unfortunately, these unhealthy boundaries and his sense of over-responsibility will not help him be a godly husband and father.

Consider a teenage daughter whose mother says, in word or action,

"If you don't become a doctor, I won't love you anymore." Perhaps this young girl believes God is calling her to be a missionary to care for orphans and to share the gospel with them. What should a daughter pursue—God's calling or her mom's desire? What would that kind of pressure on a young woman do to her thoughts about herself and to her relationship with her mom? Should a daughter be in the position of having to choose between God's will for her life or her mother's will?

Or—if a child is the center of the universe in his family for twenty-five years, what will he expect to be when he marries and has his own children? If his family did everything they could to keep him from ever being upset or ever facing difficulties head on, will he be better prepared to be a selfless, humble, servant-hearted godly man or a selfish narcissist?

Would a woman whose family spoiled her when she was young and never said no to her be well prepared for the challenges of adulthood, working at a job and respecting her boss, or being married and honoring her husband's leadership?

What kind of relationship will a mother-in-law have with her daughter-in-law if the mother-in-law has built her entire life around her son and depends on him spiritually and emotionally rather than depending on Christ? The mother may enter into a competition with his wife for her son's heart. This could bring much division and destruction to her son's marriage covenant and to her own as well, because she is interfering with God's design for her son to leave his parents and cleave to his wife (Gen. 2:24).

It would be a similar scenario for a daughter whose mom is enmeshed with her. The daughter will not be well prepared to be a godly wife and will have a hard time cutting ties with her mom to be an independent, healthy adult. She will tend to put her mom above her husband when she marries and will seek Mom's approval and leadership above her husband's approval and leadership. This creates resentment for a husband and triggers division in marriage.

My Son Can Never Be Unhappy!

Some parenting methods today advocate that it is cruel and unloving for a mom to ever allow her baby to cry for even a minute. I believe this method is harmful to moms, to marriages, and to our children. In my view, it sets up unrealistic expectations and goals that can lead to a mom idolizing her child's happiness. It can also lead to total exhaustion and nervous breakdowns for new moms.

I can certainly have goals of always seeking to meet my baby's needs to the best of my ability and to be responsible and a godly mother for him. But if my goal in being a successful mother is that my son may never cry or ever be upset, my son and I are both going to be miserable. It is not possible, nor is it healthy, for me to attempt to create a life that is completely free of any momentary discomfort for my child.

When my baby's happiness is my greatest goal, and I can't let him cry at all, I will be willing to sacrifice many things to this idol. I will sacrifice my sleep, my health, and all my time. I will sacrifice my marriage and my husband. I will sacrifice my time with God. I will probably resent my husband if he doesn't have the same perspective. If he suggests putting the baby down safely in his infant seat for a few minutes so I can take a shower, I may believe he is not a good husband or dad for daring to suggest such a thing. I become a slave to my child's contentment at every moment.

My Children Must Like Me Today, or I Will Be Crushed

If I want to be my children's best friend, and if I count on their current "approval rating" for me as a mom as my standard of measuring my success as a mom, I will create monsters. God puts parents in charge rather than children because children can't always predict what decisions will be best in the long run. As a mature adult, this is an ability I should have—or should be able to learn with God's help. If I spoil my children and try to be buddies with them all the time rather than enforcing any kind of appropriate, loving discipline, I will ruin them.

I treat them with respect and honor even now. But I am the authority, not my children. If I get confused about that, my children are intelligent enough to exploit my confusion and to take over the family. The problem is, when children are in charge of a family, there is chaos.

A child left undisciplined disgraces its mother. (Prov. 29:15)

Discipline your children, and they will give you peace;
    they will bring you the delights you desire. (Prov. 29:17)

I Can't Let Anything Bad Ever Happen to My Children

Of course I want to be responsible and do my best to take the best care of my children. But I have to accept the fact that I am not omnipotent or sovereign over my children's lives. I am not God. If I can accept this fact, I will spare myself a lot of needless anxiety. If I am able to trust God with my children and do my best to be a godly steward, I can live in peace. I know that God will cause all things to work for my best and for my children's best and for His glory in their lives—even if they do get sick or hurt and even if tragedy strikes.

This is not an easy thing to think about. But I need to decide if I am willing to trust God and His wisdom or not. I don't want to live a life of fear before my children. When I live in fear rather than faith in God, I make poor decisions. I stunt my children's spiritual and emotional growth. And sometimes, I repel my children or even push them toward the very things I fear most when I am consumed with fear over all the possible "what-ifs" in life. I want to model the kind of great faith and trust in God that I long for my children to imitate.

How Can I Tear the Idols from My Heart?

Another way to describe idolizing someone is "being enmeshed" with him or her. I have my emotions tied up in that person in an unhealthy way. I depend on that person or what he does for my contentment and happiness. When I begin to get rid of idols in my heart, a big part of that is creating healthy space between me and other people. I want to cling only to Jesus. I want to have just the right balance of space and closeness with others. But it may feel like too much space at first if I have not been giving a healthy amount of space to my children.

This can feel scary at first. It can seem as if I am being unloving if I stop idolizing my children. I have to unhook my emotions from my children's lives. I will give them things that at first may not feel like gifts to me. Room. Space. A bit more freedom to breathe and think for themselves. It can take some time to find the right balance. That is okay. It may be that my husband or a godly older mom friend may be able to help me discern finding a healthy balance here. There is also some helpful information in appendix D about healthy versus unhealthy relationships that may be a good guide.

Most importantly, I can pray. God can and will give me His wisdom and teach me His kind of love as I seek Him. He can help me notice my motives are getting offtrack as I take my thoughts captive for Him, as we discussed in chapter 3. As I have my children in a healthy place in my heart and priorities, I will find that I'm able to experience so much more of God's peace, and so will they. They may even enjoy being around me a lot more, and we might find that we're much closer in a healthy way that we could never have experienced when I idolized my children.

How Do I Lead Without Controlling and Idolizing My Children?

I think it is important to stop and look at my ultimate goals as a mother and be sure I am choosing the path that leads to the destination I truly desire for my children and myself. What do I want to see as the end result of my time with them? I know we all want our children to grow up to be healthy in every way, well adjusted, prepared to live on their own, and ready to have healthy relationships with others.

I want my children to do these things:

- Handle finances responsibly
- Know how to choose a godly spouse, if it is God's will
- Be prepared to be godly spouses
- Be prepared to be godly parents, according to God's will
- Be close to God
- Have strong, biblical morals and ethics
- Not be swayed by temptation or Satan's snares
- Obey God's Word
- Have strong, godly friends
- Make wise choices for themselves
- Hear God's voice clearly
- Follow God's will for them
- Bring Him the most glory in their lives

How can I best lead my children to embrace all these kinds of things? I can teach them with my words. I can take them to a Bible-teaching church. I can prayerfully choose the best schooling situation for them. Those can be good things. But there is no magic formula I can choose that will guarantee the outcomes I desire for my children. This journey is about living by faith.

> ## My most powerful witness to my children is my own consistent example.

The most powerful way I can encourage my children to become godly young people is to live my own life as a consistent example of holiness and godliness to them as they grow up in my home. They need to see authenticity from me, and they need to see the power of God's Spirit radically transforming my life on a daily basis. A huge part of my ability to demonstrate a godly life to them is that I don't put my children, my husband, anyone, or anything else above Christ in my own heart. At times, I may need to let my children go in certain situations—if not literally (when they are young and still at home), then at least emotionally in certain ways.

I might emotionally let go of my children when they are very young by allowing them to sleep in their own beds when the time is right. I could let them walk into the school building by themselves from the car rider line when they are old enough. Or I might let them try to handle issues at high school on their own before I step in. I can give them a bit of space and trust God to work through their teachers unless I see a big problem that needs to be addressed. I don't have to be a "helicopter parent" who hovers over everything. I can let my children handle their own homework and responsibilities, as they are able to.

> My children can't be the most
> important priority in my life. Jesus
> alone belongs in that place.

I also don't have to be a "bulldozer parent" who plows over every obstacle my children face so that they never have any problems to deal with in life. My children need to learn how to deal with some difficult, frustrating people and situations when I am not there. I can't land a job for them in the future or demand that their boss treat them fairly. There are parents who try to interfere in their grown children's work lives and marriages, but that is a destructive approach. I need to begin the process of letting them handle greater responsibility while they are still with me so that they will be ready to be independent adults one day.

As I am writing this chapter, my son is on a trip with our church student ministries to learn about leadership. I could be super upset that he is gone. I could worry myself to death over his safety and text his leader every five minutes to be sure he is alive and well. I could refuse to let him go because something bad might happen to him on a trip and I am not there to stop it. But I don't have to freak out. I can let him spread his wings and have more independence and freedom as he gets older. This will set a great pattern for how we will relate more and more as he becomes an adult.

The fact is, my children can't be the absolute most important priority in my life. Children are such good gifts from God. I can seek to bless them, love them, and be a godly mom to them as long as I live on this earth. But I can never exalt them above Christ in my life.

I PUT MY CHILDREN ABOVE EVERYTHING ELSE —STACEY'S STORY

My husband and I have wonderful children. They truly are a joy to us, but as each one was born, I spent every waking moment thinking about them, nursing them, and nurturing them. I worked extra hours at my job to afford more lessons, clubs, and toys for them, and eventually I chose to homeschool them through sixth grade.

They were my entire world, and I made the foolish assumption that they were my husband's world, too. I remember a woman from my church telling me a biblical principle that my husband should still come before the children. No way, I thought. They needed me, I rationalized.

I never imagined that by putting my husband on the back burner, our marriage would begin to crumble, brick by brick. My sex drive was low, as I was so consumed by being a mom. Our finances were low from all of their activities, and I could not rationalize spending money on date night when that money could be spent on new ballet shoes for our daughter or skating lessons for our son.

I could not figure out why my husband would want to spend his only night off from his job with me and miss out on family time. At some point, I ended up sleeping in the children's room. I guess it was because they each breastfed for a while and my husband got tired of the kids in bed with us, so I kept the peace by moving into the kids' rooms at night.

Eventually, we fought all the time and wrote nasty notes to each other when we really didn't want to speak face-to-face. And the time we did spend together was at a swim meet, ballet recital, skating competition, or other child-related activity. I had the occasional girl time with my mommy friends, and he had his guy time with, well, the guys . . . or so I thought. When we still had two children living at home, I caught him texting another woman and found that he had been having an affair for about five months. What a wake-up call. We went to our pastor and eventually made our marriage better than it has ever been.

Ah, but I digress. The lesson I learned was that although my children did need me, they also needed to see two healthy parents. I now realize that they were always watching us, and I pray that they never fall into dysfunctional relationships as they date and marry. I pray that they don't remember the loud arguments as much as they remember the trips to Six Flags. I pray that they don't remember the nasty notes on the kitchen counter as much as they remember the love notes I now write to my husband. I pray that they don't wonder why I slept in their rooms for years as much as they remember that we are a loving couple that turns the radio up nice and loud when we retire to our bedroom (wink, wink).

HAPPINESS WAS MY GREATEST IDOL —GABRIELLE'S STORY

After I began to identify a lot of my idols of wanting to feel loved, wanting attention, etc., it all started boiling down to one big idol of happiness. Happiness was the mother idol—with a bunch of little idols attached to it. I desired to be happy by being home, by my son "acting right," by my son eating healthy food, by my son staying safe, by my husband being happy and content, by my respecting and submitting to my husband, by my eating healthy and taking vitamins, by doing everything right, by having a perfectly clean home, by controlling my family, my life, and myself.

I literally set up my own happiness as my biggest goal in life, and I turned to idolizing all these other little things to try to get my idol of happiness! I realized that I had spent twenty-nine years of the precious life God gave me on trying to be happy! I looked for happiness in all the wrong places—all resulting in me *never* being happy! I imagined that if I was married, loved, and had a home, and if I could stay home and raise my son—make him behave, teach him about God, eat healthy, and just be a wife and mom—then I would be happy! I honestly even thought that if I just did whatever God says to do in the Bible, then I would be happy. I seriously wanted to be happy more than I wanted anything else in this life.

For the first time, I realized that I did not receive any joy, happiness, or contentment from being at home, from homeschooling my son, from respecting and honoring my husband, from putting my son back in public school, from keeping a clean house, from controlling (not really) my son's behavior or food choices—nor from anything the Lord had graciously given me in my life. No—I only found true joy in abiding in Christ and seeing His beautiful face! Happiness is about a passing moment. Joy—real joy—is from the Spirit of God. That is what I want—not some passing happiness. That's why I was so excited about learning about contentment, because I was freed from that idol of happiness and found so much joy in God alone! It was a *major* stepping-stone for me! To God alone be the glory!

A Painful but Important Step

As I am willing to do the painful work of tearing out any idols in my heart, and as I yield control totally to God, I discover another key to being a peaceful mom. Idols naturally bring anxiety and fear with them. When I try to fill up my deepest needs with anyone or anything other than God, I will be very disappointed. It is not that I have to take my children out of my life. It is just that my motives, thoughts, and priorities have to change to honor the Lord. When my children are not my idols, then I can more easily have the healthy relationship with them that I always wanted. I am no longer sabotaging the closeness I desire to have with them.

A Peaceful Mom's Prayer

Lord,

I am going to put 100 percent of my faith in You from now on, no matter what my family may do. You are my Rock. I want to learn to live in the sufficiency of Christ! I want to be stable and unshakable in You, even if I face my deepest fears. This is about You and me. I lay down my fears—every one of them. I name each one here before You. I acknowledge that I have been putting my desires for my children above You in my heart, and that is sin. I acknowledge my sin of unbelief in You, Lord. Please forgive me! I don't want to live like this anymore! I don't want to put anything above You in my heart. Help me tear out these idols. Help me build my life and faith on Christ, Your truth, and Your Word alone.

Amen.

Trusting God's Will for My Children

Not my will, but yours be done. (Luke 22:42)

God has plans for my family and my children—very good plans that He has known about since before the creation of the world. His plans are "good" in the sense that they ultimately result in the most possible eternal good for everyone involved and the most glory for Himself. I love my family and want what is best for them, too. Sometimes, though, I am tempted to want to put my plans for my children above God's plans. Maybe I even fear that God's plans might not really be good—or maybe His plans aren't the absolute best. Perhaps I might be tempted to think that I might really know better than He does.

Does that line of thought sound familiar? It is the same train of thought that Satan used to deceive Eve into eating the forbidden fruit. He convinced her that God was holding out on her. "God doesn't really have your best interests at heart, Eve. You have more wisdom than God does about what is best. You should decide what you want for yourself. Don't listen to God." Satan uses the same temptation with me today in so many areas. But how many times do I not even realize whose voice I am listening to?

Satan's greatest sin is pride. He wants to be equal to or above God. He whispers that same lie to me, and it sounds like my own thoughts: God doesn't love me enough, isn't wise enough, or isn't powerful enough to do what's best, so I need to take control. He entices me to believe that my wisdom is as good as, or better than, God's. He tries to convince me that if I trust God, He will ruin everything and that I am much better off if I try to do things my way (which is really Satan's way). It is as if Satan wants to convince me that my good, loving, faithful, perfect God will steal, kill, and destroy my life and family if I have faith in Him— rather than realizing that Satan is truly the one seeking to steal, kill, and destroy me and everyone I love.

A Mother's Dreams

Most of us enter motherhood with many unwritten expectations. We have a certain script in our mind of how things are "supposed to go." Some of my dreams or expectations for my children may be things like these:

- No colic or fussiness
- Perfect health
- Perfect sleeping through the night
- Only healthy foods
- An orderly schedule with set nap times, feedings, and bedtime that is never interrupted
- Popularity at school
- Good looks
- Attending a certain school or being homeschooled
- Salvation in Christ
- Long life
- The American dream
- A certain number of activities each week—like organized sports
- Specific interests

- Perfect character and emotional/spiritual maturity
- Certain weight and size
- Intelligence and all As in school
- Athleticism and winning awards in sports
- Musical ability
- A certain group of friends
- A specific personality
- A certain college or career path
- Marriage by a certain age
- A certain kind of spouse
- Grandkids by a certain time
- A specific number of phone calls/emails/texts per week when they are in college or beyond
- A certain standard of living when they are on their own

The reality is that I don't have control over all these things. I may believe that something is best for my child—but I may not be able to make it happen. Sometimes, what I think is best may not even ultimately be what is best. I can't see into the future. I am not sovereign or omniscient. My ability to know what is best is pretty limited.

When I Don't Trust

I personally spent many years not fully trusting God with my family and my life. I said I trusted God, but I held a lot of things back and tried to handle them on my own. What misery I created for my loved ones and myself!

When I choose to trust myself rather than the Lord, things do not go well with me spiritually because I am not in right relationship with God. I'm pushing Him off the throne and trying to usurp His authority. And when I am trying to be God, I don't have the ability to be in right relationship with other people, either. I end up with loneliness, frustration, resentment, worry, and fear.

And without faith it is impossible to please God, because anyone who comes to him must believe that he exists and that he
rewards those who earnestly seek him. (Heb. 11:6)

I didn't really understand this for so long. God rewards those who
fully trust Him. (It is not that He necessarily gives us all the mate-
rial things we want. He is a good father, not an indulgent one.) He
does not reward those who don't have faith in Him, who essentially
believe God is a liar. Lack of faith in God is the same thing as pride—
thinking I can do it better. I trust myself more than I trust God. God
gives Himself fully to those who put all their faith in Him. He stands
against those who trust anything or anyone but Him. As James writes,
"God opposes the proud but shows favor to the humble" (4:6).

"God wants me to be right with Him more than anything else."

I will experience God's loving discipline if I belong to Him and I
have pride (Heb. 12:5–6). He wants me to see my wrong attitudes, to
humble myself, and to repent. He wants to restore me to a right relationship with Him. He may use some painful situations to open my
eyes to my lack of faith, because my repentance is the most important
thing to Him. God wants me to be right with Him more than anything
else.

If I don't trust God at all, I forfeit all of God's promises because I do
not belong to Him (John 3:18). But even as a believer in Christ, I may
lack faith. I may struggle with doubts and unbelief.

Some consequences of my not trusting God could include these:

- God won't answer my prayers (James 1:5–8).
- I won't have the power of the Holy Spirit (Eph. 4:30).
- I miss out on much of God's provision (Num. 14:2–11, 20–24).

- I forfeit God's conditional promises (Matt. 6:33).
- I won't have His peace (Isa. 59:8).
- I won't have the fruit of His Spirit (Gal. 5:22–23).
- I won't be able to rightly discern and know His will for me (Prov. 3:5–6).
- I take myself out from under God's protection and place myself in danger (Ps. 91:1–4).
- I inadvertently trust Satan and his lies and become easy prey for him (1 Peter 5:8–9).
- I miss God's presence, fellowship, and miracles (Mark 6:4–6).

I think about myself as a parent, even though I am far from perfect. I truly do love my children. When I ask my children not to do certain things, it is almost always because I love them and want to protect them from harm. Or it is because I want them to receive something good that will be for their benefit. Children don't have the wisdom to know what is best for them in the moment. They need the wise, loving guidance and provision of their parents.

> Which of you fathers, if your son asks for a fish, will give him a snake instead? Or if he asks for an egg, will give him a scorpion? If you then, though you are evil, know how to give good gifts to your children, how much more will your Father in heaven give the Holy Spirit to those who ask him! (Luke 11:11–13)

Imagine what tragedies might result if my children decided not to trust while they were still young enough to be under my care. They might end up experiencing a lot of dangerous, awful things that I could have easily prevented. They may also miss out on so many good things I could have provided. Their health, safety, grades, relationships, and ability to become responsible adults, as well as their chance to experience some fun and adventures I would like to give them, depend on their willingness to trust and obey their parents.

WHY I CAN TRUST

Thankfully, God doesn't expect me to blindly trust Him. He gives me plenty of concrete evidence about His character, His existence, and the trustworthiness of the Bible. Then I can base my trust on facts and truth. The more I know Him, the more I realize that I have every reason to trust Him.

Here are some resources that can help me discover how I can know beyond any doubt that the Bible is true and that God is real:

- John Piper's website (www.desiringgod.org)—sermons and articles such as "Do You Ever Doubt God's Existence?" and "How Can You Know the Bible Is True?" by a trusted pastor.
- Answers in Genesis—biblical answers to questions about the existence of God (answersingenesis.org/god/), scientific evidence for the creation story in Genesis (answersingenesis.org/evidence -for-creation/), and scientific evidence against evolution (answers ingenesis.org/evidence-against-evolution/).
- Josh McDowell's website (www.josh.org/resources/apologetics/) and books—biblical answers to questions about the authenticity, reliability, and truth of the Bible, written by a former atheist who has come to Christ. Evidence for the existence of God and the truth about the identity of Jesus as the Christ.

When I get to know who God is and His character, the reasons why I can trust Him become abundantly clear.

God Is Worthy of My Trust

Once I am clear on the fact that the Bible is true and trustworthy, I can believe the things that Scripture says about God. I can know that the way the Lord presents Himself in the Bible is an accurate representation of His character. And if the God of the Bible exists and is who the Bible claims He is, He is absolutely worthy of all my trust. In fact, I would be crazy *not* to trust Him.

- He keeps all His promises.
- He can't lie.
- He is perfect.
- He is the very embodiment of love.
- He is the source of absolute truth.
- He is incapable of any evil.
- He is completely good.
- He is the source of all real wisdom.
- He is just and takes vengeance on all sin and evil.
- He is the Creator and sustainer of the universe.
- He extends grace to sinners through Jesus and the cross.
- He was willing to become human and die in my place so I can be with Him.

If a God like the Bible describes exists, how could I not trust such a one? If I can't trust the only being in the entire universe who is completely good, who can only act in love toward me, who took on the punishment I deserved for my sin, who could I trust?

No One Else Is Worthy of All My Trust

When I clearly see who God is and that His word is true, I also have to come face-to-face with the fact that there is no other person or being who is perfect, who has all wisdom, who only always acts in love. I have to acknowledge that I am far from being as trustworthy as God. I don't have all wisdom. I am not always good and loving. No human can ever remotely live up to the perfection that is in God's character.

God's Word shines light on this decision and makes it very easy.

- Do I trust the one and only God who is always good, wise, and loving and who is completely worthy of all I can give Him?
- Do I trust someone or something else who will fail me and who is not worthy of my faith and trust?

What God Will Do

God doesn't ask me to have a relationship with Him for nothing. He promises that if I seek Him wholeheartedly, I am not wasting my time.

> I have not spoken in secret,
>   from somewhere in a land of darkness;
>   I have not said . . .
>   "Seek me in vain."
>   I, the LORD, speak the truth;
>   I declare what is right. (Isa. 45:19)

What does it mean for me to have a close relationship with Him that is built on trust? One of the easiest ways for me to see what my relationship with God could be like is to see what my relationship with my loving earthly father is like. The Lord provides a father-daughter relationship to help me wrap my mind around what His love for me looks like in tangible ways.

God Is a Loving Parent

My earthly parents can never be as perfect as my heavenly Father, but if I had a plugged-in earthly father, especially one who loved me when I was growing up, even if he wasn't a believer, I can see parallels that help me catch a glimpse of God's design for my relationship with Him.

Like a good earthly father, the Lord does many things for me:

- Provides for my true needs
- Leads me in paths that are ultimately best for me

- Speaks to me in words of love, encouragement, rebuke, instruction, and wisdom
- Enjoys being with me
- Desires to bless me
- Loves to hear my heart
- Wants to know me
- Wants me to know His heart
- Protects me

God Provides for Me as Lord

When I think of God as "Daddy," I see more of His heart for me. But His love and provision for me go so far beyond any earthly relationship.

God wants to do these things for me:

- Save me from eternal condemnation (2 Peter 3:9)
- Cleanse me from all sin and wrongdoing (Ps. 51:2)
- Completely transform my heart and mind (Rom. 12:1–2)
- Love me completely with His perfect love (1 Cor. 13:4–8)
- Let me enjoy and delight in His presence (Ps. 37:4)
- Give His good plan for my life to me to enjoy (Jer. 29:11–13)
- Give me peace with Him (Rom. 5:1)
- Listen to my heart (Ps. 62:8)
- Receive my wholehearted love for Him (Matt. 22:37)
- Speak to me through His Word and His Spirit (2 Tim. 3:16)
- Provide thousands of promises for me (2 Peter 1:4)
- Protect me from Satan's plans to destroy me (2 Thess. 3:3)
- Give me victory over temptation and evil (1 Cor. 15:57)
- Fight for me against my enemies (Exod. 14:14)
- Heal my brokenness (Ps. 147:3)
- Create a unique and beautiful masterpiece of my life (Isa. 61:3)
- Provide real security, acceptance, and purpose in my life (1 John 4:18)

- Be united with me spiritually (1 Cor. 6:17)
- Guide me in my decisions in life (Isa. 30:21)
- Provide for my needs and be my source and supply (Phil. 4:19)
- Share my life with me (Rev. 3:20)
- Refine me to make me more and more like Jesus (James 1:1–4)
- Do all the spiritual heavy lifting and hard work for me (Rom. 5:17)
- Give real rest to my soul (Matt. 11:28–30)
- Rejoice and sing over me in love (Zeph. 3:17)
- Share heaven with me forever (Rev. 22:1–5)
- Be my greatest treasure (Gen. 15:1)

God Leads in Mysterious Ways

The way I relate to God when I don't get what I think I want at the moment is very telling about how much I trust Him. All of us will face things that throw us off balance and that test us. When things are going along with my will, life seems so easy. But when I have my heart set on something and then I don't receive it or things don't go as I planned, I have a choice to make. Will I try to do things my way, or will I entrust myself to the Lord's will, whatever it may be? Whatever the cost? That is true discipleship, and this attitude is a key to living in God's indescribable peace.

Sometimes it is only by my taking God's path, even when it doesn't look good to me at the time, that I find what is best. I could never have understood—at the time—what God was doing in Joseph's life in Genesis when his brothers sold him into slavery, and he spent years as a slave and a prisoner (though he was innocent of any crime). I would have struggled to believe that God would exalt him to second-in-command in Egypt and use him to save countless people from starvation.

Could I have walked beside Job in his suffering when he lost all of his children and possessions in one day, or wrap my mind around the way God would use his story and faith to teach and bless millions of people for thousands of years? I'm also not sure I could have looked past the agony and suffering of Jesus on the cross to see the healing, salvation, and blessing that would come to millions and millions of people through Jesus's obedience to God.

I couldn't even see God's hand in my daddy getting transferred from Pittsburgh, Pennsylvania, to Columbia, South Carolina, when I was fourteen. How I cried about what a terrible thing it was that we had to move so far away. I had to leave my church, my friends, my school, and my neighborhood. I had to abandon my plans and dreams for my life at the time. But it turns out God knew what He was doing. That move was exactly what our family needed—for each of us—in ways we couldn't have imagined beforehand.

> The way I relate to God when
> I don't get what I want is very
> telling about my trust in Him.

Often it is only as I look back after the fact that I can see how God's hand was lovingly leading me, even in the things I didn't like at the time. I may be thinking about the next year or the next few decades. I may have just my little family's life in mind. But God is thinking about much bigger things. When my dreams and plans for my children or my life seem to be crumbling at my feet, I want to respond with all the more faith! He may be leading us in exactly the way that will accomplish the very best for us in the end.

The more I know God, the more I can trust Him. And the more I trust Him, the more He is willing to reveal to me of His will for my life. When I don't trust Him, I miss out on so many of His blessings and miracles. But when I walk by faith in Him, He loves to direct my steps and give me the light I need for each moment. I have tasted enough of His goodness to know that I don't want to miss out on Him or anything He wants to give me ever again!

A HANDICAP BROUGHT MANY BLESSINGS
—MY STORY (WITH MY FATHER'S PERMISSION)

When my father was born in 1942, the doctor didn't expect him to live. The doctor was also very busy trying to save my grandmother, who was not expected to survive, either. So my father didn't receive the treatment he needed for his exposure to toxoplasmosis—a bacterial infection his mom had acquired, most likely from having contact with contaminated cat litter. My grandmother and father both survived and are still both alive and well today. But my father subsequently lost vision in the center of his right eye, and he lost his hearing in his left ear.

My father moved to Mississippi his senior year of high school because my grandfather retired from the Coast Guard and decided to move his family there from Connecticut. My father had a few dozen people in his class, and the superintendent at Ocean Springs School District really went out of his way to help his students there. My grandparents didn't have money for their sons to go to college. But then this superintendent researched scholarships and found one for my father based on physical handicaps—a scholarship he could not have received if they had still been in Connecticut.

In college, my dad had to take ROTC with Mississippi State. His plan was to continue on into the military and to join a new program called the Green Beret. He found out when he got his physical for advanced ROTC that he would not be accepted into advanced ROTC or the military due to his hearing and vision loss. He would have almost certainly gone to Vietnam had he been accepted.

It is amazing to me that God used my father's situation—the lack of proper medical care as a newborn and the complications he suffered from that—to allow him to go to a four-year college in the early 1960s. He majored in nuclear engineering. Later, he helped to design nuclear submarines for the US government, and then he worked for Westinghouse for many years.

Because of my father's job, he moved to Pittsburgh, where he met my mother. And later, because of his nuclear engineering job, our family was transferred to Columbia, South Carolina, in 1987. The next year, I met Greg, my husband.

It is often only in hindsight that we can see God's hand at work. How thankful I am to see God accomplishing His will in mysterious ways in my life, my family members' lives, and in the lives of all believers in Christ. We can't begin to understand it all at the time, but as we trust the Lord, He will reveal His purposes in time.

THE SCHOOL MADE A BIG MISTAKE —MY STORY

Our son had applied to the Quest program when he was in eighth grade. Quest is an advanced placement program at his high school that is extremely academically rigorous. He filled out the application and spent several days writing essays that spring semester. His guidance counselor was absent the day he turned in his application, so he gave it to another lady in the office, and she promised to give it to the guidance counselor.

Months passed. We heard nothing from the school until two weeks before his ninth-grade year started. Our son had been placed in the STEM (science, technology, engineering, and mathematics) program rather than the Quest program. It is still an honors program, but there is not as much college credit available in the STEM program as in Quest.

We were confused, so I took him to the high school and respectfully asked to speak to someone about why he was put in a different program. The vice principal brought out his application and told us they had never received his essays. This was probably three to four months after he had turned them in. At this point, there was no room in the Quest program anymore. The administrator suggested that he try the STEM program for two weeks to see if he liked it. She said, "Sometimes things happen for a reason." It was tempting for me to be upset with the school for botching our son's application to Quest. But then there seemed to be no alternative at this point but to try the STEM program.

I prayed with my son for God's will. We talked about how perhaps this happened because God was leading him this way and it would ultimately be a better choice for him. Instead of getting upset, we were able to look for God's hand in the situation.

Now he has been in the program for two years, and he loves it! It turns out to be the best possible fit for him. He loves his teachers. He gets the newest facilities that were recently renovated at a school that is over one hundred years old. His class has the best and newest technology of anyone in the school. He has made some new friends.

I am excited to see how God ends up using this "mistake" for good in our son's life and how He may use it to impact his entire high school career, his choice of friends, and even his career path in the future. What a blessing to serve a sovereign God and to rest in His love and sovereignty, even when I don't know what the outcome will be. God has His ways of leading me and my family as we seek His will wholeheartedly.

ENTRUSTING GROWN PRODIGAL CHILDREN TO GOD —TRICIA'S AND MARIE'S STORIES

Tricia

I am a mom of three grown children. Although they were raised in a Christian home and loved going to church as they grew up, at this time they have all chosen to opt out of embracing a personal relationship with the Lord. I realize that He doesn't want to force my children to engage with Him. He wants it to come from their hearts.

There have been times when I felt like I wasted my time by providing a spiritually rich environment during their upbringing. However, I have concluded that the Lord purposefully allowed me to be in their lives, and I do not regret the childhood that was provided to them, regardless of what they chose to do with it when they became adults. It is sad to watch the people you love living a life that is not what you wanted for them. I have chosen to not take it personally, though. I can rest in knowing that I did what I was led by the Lord to do as I raised them. I cannot "own" their spiritual choices. Each of us needs to make our own decision to have a relationship with the Lord. All we are called to do is direct those we come in contact with to the Lord and trust Him with the result. I will claim this promise from Scripture. The New Living Translation paraphrases Isaiah 49:4 beautifully when it says: "My work seems so useless! I have spent my strength for nothing and to no purpose. Yet I will leave it all in the LORD's hand; I will trust God for my reward." On the outside, what I've accomplished may not have seemed fruitful, but my leaving everything in the Lord's hand is the best thing for me to do, trusting Him with the results.

Marie

One of the hardest things I ever had to do was lay down my fear that my children would never walk with the Lord again when they both proclaimed to be atheists. I had homeschooled them and brought them up knowing the Lord. How could they turn from Him?

Life has been tougher than it should have been in our home, and the children reacted by blaming God for not answering their prayers that it get better. I understood their pain. I had at one dark point in my own adult life walked away from God. My children did not know of this, but it helped me understand their choice. It was with that understanding that I knew I had to leave their hearts with God.

My babies! How could I not fight for them? The answer was that it was God's fight, not mine. I remembered that ultimately they are His children first, and He loves them more than I ever could. He wants them back under His mighty arms, too, but He has life lessons for them just as He does for me. When I walked away, it was important to my journey. I trust that what they are going through is equally important to theirs. The Lord knows what is best for them, so I leave them in His very capable hands.

What I offer to them is unconditional love. I let them know we will agree to disagree at times but that Mom and Dad are here for anything they need. That knowledge and love has made us a stronger family. If I pushed faith on them, I would push them away. This way I am a part of their lives, and they feel their independence as adults is real, and no strings attached. Then I live my faith out to them through loving them as Jesus does.

Elisabeth Elliot experienced incredible tragedy when her young husband, Jim, was martyred by the Huaorani tribe in Ecuador. God later used her to bring the gospel and the love of Christ to the very people who murdered her husband and his team. Her words about letting go and entrusting everything to God carry great weight for us all.

There is no ongoing spiritual life without this process of letting go. At the precise point where we refuse, growth stops. If we hold tightly to anything given to us, unwilling to let it go when the time comes to let it go or unwilling to allow it to be used as the Giver means it to be used, we stunt the growth of the soul.

It is easy to make a mistake here. "If God gave it to me," we say, "it's mine. I can do what I want with it." No. The truth is that it is ours to thank Him for and ours to offer back to Him, ours to relinquish, ours to lose, ours to let go of—*if* we want to find our true selves, if we want real Life, if our hearts are set on glory.[4]

How Can I Learn Practically to Trust God?

All this talk about trusting God makes releasing control seem a little simple. I know that it isn't.

It helped me to learn to trust God more fully if I traced my two hands palms up on a piece of paper, so that my hands were in a position of giving everything to God. Then I listed all the things that were dear to me on the fingers of each hand, such as my husband, children, health, money, career, house, future, and death. I decided to give these things completely to God to use however He thought was best. When I didn't really "get" how good God was, it was so scary to trust Him with all these things. But then, as He began to show me how faithful and good He is, I began to see that this was the best place to be in the world.

I want to have all of His will now and nothing but His will—whatever that may be. Thankfully, He is more than willing to show me His way if only I will follow and trust Him.

Whether you turn to the right or to the left, your ears will hear a voice behind you, saying, "This is the way; walk in it." (Isa. 30:21)

This is what the LORD says . . .
  "I am the LORD your God,
  who teaches you what is best for you,

who directs you in the way you should go.
If only you had paid attention to my commands,
your peace would have been like a river,
your well-being like the waves of the sea." (Isa. 48:17–18)

A Peaceful Mom's Prayer

Lord,

You are the sovereign, almighty King of the entire universe. You alone are worthy of all praise. You alone are worthy of all sacrifice, worship, and trust. I want Your will—all Your will— and nothing but Your will for me, for my husband, and for our children. Whatever it takes. Whatever the cost. I don't have to know what You are up to. I trust You. I desire You more than anything or anyone in this life. I seek only Your pleasure and Your glory. Use my life and my family to bring great honor to Your name and to bring many into Your kingdom. Help me to understand that trusting You is wise and trusting anyone or anything else is terrifying. If You are with me, I have everything that really matters!

Amen!

Seeing Through the Lens of Eternity

Store up for yourselves treasures in heaven.
(Matthew 6:20)

Humans are prone to focus on the here and now. I like everything to make sense to me at the moment. So many of my trust issues and my struggles with making my children idols are because I'm caught up in the urgent things calling for my attention. I may be tempted to want what seems to be "the best thing" to make my children or myself happy in this fleeting moment.

But God gently, lovingly calls me to enter into His majestic throne room in the highest heavens to see things from His eternal perspective in which "a day is like a thousand years, and a thousand years are like a day" (2 Peter 3:8). He calls me to see what things will truly matter one thousand years from now, one billion years from now, and for eons to come after that.

So I may be right that my children need to

Eat their vegetables   Clean up their rooms
Avoid too much junk food   Make their beds

Use good manners

Get enough exercise

Wear a coat when it is cold
   outside

Get enough sleep each night

Do all their chores

Earn good grades

Have godly friends

Speak respectfully to me

Finish their homework

Be on time getting out the
   door

Limit their screen time

Date only godly people

But what if, in focusing on these good things, I forget about things that are *most* important from God's perspective? It is sobering to me that if I make these issues on the list most important, I may feel I am justified to sin against my children in order to get them to do what I think they should do. I may feel entitled to lose my temper, disrespect them, or insult them to try to motivate them to do what I think they should do. I may believe that because the results I want are good, "the ends justify the means." But this is not how our holy God thinks or works.

"What if, in focusing on these good things, I forget about things that are *most* important?"

God never justifies anyone's sin. The ends do not justify the means in God's eyes. He is interested in my character, my motives, and my attitudes every moment. Those are the things He will hold me accountable for when I stand before Him—not whether my child was perfectly potty trained at age two. I won't get a heavenly reward from God because my child's report card was perfect or because we were only late getting to school three times in second grade. He is going to uncover the hidden motives of my heart (1 Cor. 4:5).

So while I do want to get certain things done and these things are somewhat important, I know I have to keep my eye on the real prize, which is God's approval and pleasure. He will reward me in heaven for my obedience to Him, and I will get to cherish those rewards forever!

> So neither the one who plants nor the one who waters is anything, but only God, who makes things grow. The one who plants and the one who waters have one purpose, and they will each be rewarded according to their own labor. For we are co-workers in God's service; you are God's field, God's building.
>
> By the grace God has given me, I laid a foundation as a wise builder, and someone else is building on it. But each one should build with care. For no one can lay any foundation other than the one already laid, which is Jesus Christ. If anyone builds on this foundation using gold, silver, costly stones, wood, hay or straw, their work will be shown for what it is, because the Day will bring it to light. It will be revealed with fire, and the fire will test the quality of each person's work. If what has been built survives, the builder will receive a reward. If it is burned up, the builder will suffer loss but yet will be saved—even though only as one escaping through the flames. (1 Cor. 3:7–15)

God is most interested in how I'm building up my children to know and love Him and to love others. *How* I build and *what* I build matters. Things I build out of my flesh and my wisdom won't survive the fire. But anything built by the power of the Holy Spirit will! I want to bring my children with me as my "treasures in heaven," and I want to build well in their lives and in my own on the foundation of Jesus Christ. If I can remember my purpose—to love God, to bring glory to Him, to be a godly steward of the gifts He's given me, to love others—it'll help me keep eternal things dear to my heart, and worldly things will fade in importance.

> For to me, to live is Christ and to die is gain. If I am to go on living in the body, this will mean fruitful labor for me. Yet what

shall I choose? I do not know! I am torn between the two: I desire to depart and be with Christ, which is better by far; but it is more necessary for you that I remain in the body. Convinced of this, I know that I will remain, and I will continue with all of you for your progress and joy in the faith, so that through my being with you again your boasting in Christ Jesus will abound on account of me. (Phil. 1:21–26)

The Messy Foyer Example

I may want my children to clean up the foyer and put their shoes and book bags away. That is a good thing for a mother to be concerned about. But if I approach them with hateful glares, impatient sighs, name-calling, or yelling, what have I ultimately accomplished that will please God? Is God seriously more concerned about chores being done exactly right than about how I love my children and how I treat them? How might I learn to have an eternal perspective?

I may want to ask myself questions like these:

- How will God grade my children on how neat the foyer was today? Will this truly matter one hundred years from now?
- How will God judge my attitudes, motives, words, and behaviors toward my children? Will these things matter when I am gone—to my children?
- How does God measure my love for Him in the ways I treat my children?
- Is there a way for me to accomplish this earthly task that will bless my children and also strengthen my own walk with Christ spiritually?
- Do I want my children to remember that having everything clean was the most important thing, even if it meant that I sinned against them? Or do I want them primarily to remember feeling loved, safe, and cherished when they were with me?

It's fine to want the foyer to be straightened up, but not at the expense of things that will matter most to God and things that are life-giving to my children. I can ask my children to do what I would like them to do calmly, in a pleasant tone of voice. Even when they disobey, I can respond without sinning myself. I can be firm and respectful with my children if they disobey, and my motive can be God's love and His priorities in their lives.

I don't have to scream or curse at them and completely lose control of my mouth. I don't have to humiliate them. I can simply say, in a respectful, pleasant tone of voice, "Please clean up your shoes and book bags now. Thank you." If my children start to argue, I can address their back-talking respectfully. I can also administer any necessary discipline lovingly, gently, firmly, and with self-control as God's Spirit empowers me to do so. If they continue to rebel against my God-given authority, I may need to have my children take a time-out so they can calm down and I can pray. Or I may pray right there out loud in front of them in humility, crying out to my Father in heaven about the needs of my children's souls. I have done this many times. I need His wisdom and power every moment! This helps me be a peaceful mom.

If I realize that having a room cleaned up has become more important to me than my relationship with Christ or my relationship with my children and their emotional and spiritual well-being, I need to confess this to God and turn away from it. I need to ask Him to transform my thinking so that I am not consumed by perfectionism or by these little things that aren't going to ultimately be very important. I can ask Him to give me His perspective in the daily activities of motherhood and life.

Leaving a Godly Legacy

I believe it is wise to consider what I want my children to remember about me. Most likely, they will outlive me. What will they remember most from their time spent in my care? Will they remember, "Mom was angry a lot"? Or will they remember, "Mom got so upset if a glass broke. Glasses were really important to her"? Or will they remember lots of laughter, affection, kindness, grace, wisdom, joy, and peace in our home?

If I am thinking about what will matter in light of eternity, my character and the way I treat people will be what matters most to the Lord. One day I will stand before Him, and He will rightly judge the quality of the spiritual building I have done in my life (1 Cor. 3:10–15). A great way to measure whether I'm on track is to think about what I really want my children to remember about me. This could be a great exercise to do during your quiet time this week. Take a piece of paper or your prayer journal and write down all the things you don't want your children to remember about you and all the things you do want your children to most remember about you.

Things I want to leave as a legacy to my children include these:

- Patience
- Gentleness
- Positivity
- Big faith in Christ
- Fervent prayers
- Lots of smiles
- Laughter
- Cherished memories
- Wise instruction from God's Word
- A godly example of femininity
- Godly stewardship
- Joy
- Peace
- Forgiveness
- Grace
- A strong marriage (as much as it depends on me)

- Enjoying time together
- Warm affection

There may be other things as well that you want to pass on to them. Maybe not everything would be overtly spiritual. You may want to give them a legacy of having yummy meals together as a family or of going on walks together in the woods. You may decide to make certain occasions special with unique family traditions. There are so many ways we can leave a beautiful legacy to our children spiritually and relationally as we show them the paths that lead to peace. It is as we do simple things together with our children that we can best live out our love and godliness in tangible ways that they can receive, relate to, and cherish forever. We are in positions to impact our children in powerful ways they will never forget.

> ## "What my children need is for me to be filled up with Jesus."

I can't wait to see how God will equip each of us to bless our children and to become the moms, wives, and women He calls us to be. I may not be able to take my children on every trip I would like to or to buy them the latest styles from the most expensive clothing stores. I may not have the most luxurious house or the fanciest car. But those are not the things that create a godly legacy.

What my children need is for me to be filled up with Jesus and to let all of Him and all of myself overflow into their lives to bless them. They need to see me authentically living out my faith and continually being transformed by the power of God. As I seek to demonstrate a godly example, share things that God has taught me, answer their questions to the best of my ability, and teach Scripture to them, they will have the opportunity to choose to receive these good things, too. Then we may get to be a peaceful family together.

LEAVING MY CHILDREN A HEALTHIER LEGACY THAN WHAT WAS GIVEN TO ME —RACHEL'S STORY

My situation is one of the most extreme. My relationship with my mother was one of the most toxic. She was full of bitterness, hatred, unforgiveness, negativity, and so much toxicity that it spewed from her regularly. I was her target most of the time. Our relationship continued to erode despite my best efforts and deep desire to connect and bond with her.

It eventually reached a point where she decided she didn't want me as her daughter anymore. To say that this was damaging is like saying the ocean is a little bit of water. It's a vast understatement. If you've been through something similar, then you can relate. But you *can* overcome this and come out better on the other side. You can also stop the cycle so you don't pass it on to your own children.

Here are some lessons I learned about stopping the cycle.

1. Feel your emotions. Going through something like this is traumatic. I've often felt like my mother disowning me was like a death. I lost my mom. I didn't lose her through death but through her own choice to reject me. It was as final as death—she walked out of my life forever. The only difference was that there were no cards, no flowers, no food or comforting words from friends and acquaintances, because very few knew what I was going through. But I very much grieved the loss of my mother. And while that was painful, it was also very real and very necessary.

Stuffing your emotions down will only backfire later. You have to deal with your emotions at some point. Now is better than later. Allow yourself to grieve for what you wish you'd had and needed. It's okay to acknowledge your needs weren't met.

Your situation may not be as extreme. You may still have some contact with your toxic parent. But you still need to allow yourself to feel your emotions instead of denying them. You can't move on until you go through your emotions.

2. Treat yourself kindly. Going through an experience with a toxic parent is damaging. Acknowledge that what you've been through isn't easy. Treat yourself with kindness. Comfort yourself and encourage your own heart! Do little things such as treating yourself to your favorite coffee drink or a nap. Little niceties seem small but are actually extra important when you're going through an emotional upheaval. Most importantly, speak Scripture to yourself to overwrite Satan's lies. Instead of thinking, "I'm so stupid," replace that lie with, "I am fearfully and wonderfully made" (Ps. 139:14).

3. Give yourself time. You don't truly get over an experience like this. The scars will always be there, but they won't always be as fresh. Wounds do heal, but it takes time. Remind yourself that time will help when you feel discouraged—that time is a great healer.

4. Acknowledge the blessings of having a toxic parent. This one sounds rather horrific, but there actually are blessings that come from this situation. You realize exactly what you don't want to be. You learn a lot of lessons of self-discovery. You become stronger. You can draw closer to God. You see firsthand what seeds of complaining and ungratefulness can grow into. It's a good lesson to turn your focus to gratitude and positivity in your own life.

5. Find a new focus and start a new chapter. I think it's really important to state that what you've been through will always be with you and there will always be times you feel a twinge of hurt or sadness. That's to be expected. Completely getting over a toxic parent isn't possible. Coming to terms with it and reaching a place of acceptance is. When you finally get to a place of acceptance— and don't rush this process, or you'll have to back up and do it again—find a new focus in your life. This can be anything. For me, it was finding a hobby I loved and a job change. It'll look different for everyone, and that's okay. Starting a new chapter without carrying the burden of a traumatic relationship is so healing. You feel like you're moving into a bright future, and that's such a gift!

6. *Be honest with your children.* I've always believed in being honest with my children. I also believe you should tailor that honesty to a child's specific age so you're not giving them more than they can handle. But honesty will bond you to your children. My children are teenagers and are fully aware of what happened in my situation. Not only did I lose my mother, but they also lost a grandmother. I've always strived to be open about talking about this, encouraging them to share their feelings (because they went through something significant, too) and what this means. I also tell them that I'm doing the best I can as a mom, but I didn't have a good role model, so there are times I'm "winging" it. I ask them to forgive me if I make mistakes and assure them I'm doing the best I can. I also assure them my love for them is never in short supply.

7. *Ask God to fill in the gaps.* Lastly, I ask God to fill in the gaps. I'll never be a perfect mother. Even if I'd had an amazing example, I couldn't be perfect because that's not possible. And because I did not have a good example, being a godly mother feels even more difficult. I literally don't know the best way to handle certain situations with my children. I go on gut and God. I ask Him to fill in any gaps I may have missed in parenting. And I trust Him to take my best efforts, which still fall short sometimes, and make them His best for my children.

WHAT MY CHILDREN NEED MOST —FAITH'S STORY

I have a twenty-one-year-old and a nineteen-year-old. What I continue to learn is that the first thing to take a hit when I am under stress is my taking time to express genuine, gentle love. I know, as a parent, leading is so important and that at its very best, it looks most like discipleship. But sometimes all our fears of what will happen if we don't do everything perfectly create needless stress upon stress. Even when they're standoffish, our kids need me to draw near.

I have hover issues and a huge desire to avert disaster by trying to over-infuse wisdom. What I'm finding they need, more than I ever realized, is for me to listen to them, listen to their music, and be present, watching their successes and encouraging them when they feel like failures. Children can be so down on themselves, even more fearful than I am, seeing all of their perceived deficits. When you're in doubt, remember your encouraging words have a lot of pull with their difficult little hearts.

THE BBQ SAUCE FIASCO —SHANNON'S STORY
(SHANNON POPKIN, AUTHOR OF CONTROL GIRL)

Several days ago, child A ate a plateful of chicken nuggets in the van on the way to practice. When he got out, he left the plate with its giant puddle of BBQ sauce on the floor of the van.

Since my kids no longer need me to buckle them in, I don't often get to the back seats, and I tend to be oblivious to the mess back there. When I *do* happen to look back, as I did last night, I'm usually dismayed by what I see. This time there was McDonald's trash littered about, several pairs of socks, and the plate.

I asked child A to throw away the trash and then bring the other things inside once we got home. I guess he forgot about the second part, because this morning when I took child B to school, the socks and plate were still there.

When we pulled into the parking lot, I went to wrestle child B's backpack up from the back seat (those things are the size of a small child). And that's when I realized that it had been sitting on the plate.

"Oh, gross!" I said with great disgust and started fishing for wet wipes. But child B just slung the backpack onto his back and started walking away. I said, "Wait! It might have BBQ sauce on it . . ." He cavalierly said, "It does," and turned to display the giant smear across his bag.

I was incredulous. "Don't you want me to wipe it off for you?" I asked. He shrugged nonchalantly and rotated the bag my way. Three wet wipes later, the bag still looked dingy, but at least he wasn't going to get sauce all over the next twenty kids he bumped in the hallway.

As I drove home, my mind drifted to ways I need to prevent situations like this. Maybe I could make a rule about no eating in the car. Or at least no sauce in the car? Or maybe a rule about picking up your plate. And I needed to talk to my son about being considerate! Seriously? He was going to walk into school with sauce dripping from his back? Who does that? Apparently child B does.

I started getting really frustrated. Then angry. By the time the traffic light turned, I was fuming. *I talk and talk and make rule after rule, but nothing changes!* My mind jumped forward a decade or two. What will these kids become? Will they ever be able to keep a job? What if they never do take responsibility for themselves? Does this mean that I have been irresponsible? I get the feeling that child B's teacher thinks so. Is it true? Am I failing as their mom?

I gripped the steering wheel, deciding, *I need to clamp down, put the pressure on, and turn the heat up!*

As I screeched into the neighborhood, my blood pressure high, a thought flickered through my mind. It's the lesson that God has been teaching and re-teaching me for so long. It goes like this:

· I can't control my kids.
· Even with my most concerted control-girl efforts, I cannot forge them into considerate, responsible people.

- I can't ultimately make them pick up, clean up, or finish up.
- But I *can* look up.

There is One who ultimately is in control of my kids' futures. He has given these children to me for a short time, and He does expect me to train and influence them. *But He never asked me to control them.* And ironically, when I get angry and rant or shame or jab my finger in their faces (which I probably would have been doing had they been in the car with me at this instance), I'm failing to control the one person God actually *does* want me to control—myself!

Yes, God wants me to get my kids ready for life, but He wants me to do this through influence, not control. And the best way to influence is not lecturing through clenched teeth and trumped-up consequences; it's by *being* the type of person I'd like them to mimic.

Am I kind? Am I gentle and patient? Am I self-controlled? These are the ways the Spirit wants to influence *me*. And only when I'm under *His* influence is it possible for me to influence my kids well.

So I say, walk by the Spirit, and you will not gratify the desires of the flesh. (Gal. 5:16)

My life will probably be littered with plenty of BBQ sauce and dirty socks in the days to come. But these are moments to teach and influence, not control.

EFFECTIVE PRAYER HELPS US KEEP ETERNAL PERSPECTIVE

Prayer really is the most incredible privilege I have as a child of God in Christ! In prayer, I can stand on spiritual tiptoes to catch a vision of what He may want to accomplish that earthly eyes cannot see in a difficult situation. I start to accept God's timetable instead of my own, recognizing that He is not limited by time or space. The more I pray in faith, the more I grow in faith and the more I can see with His eyes, love with His heart, and act with His mind.

Prayer is my way of communicating with God, focusing my attention on Him—His desires, His goals, His eternity. It is about my relationship with Him, spiritual and emotional intimacy together. Prayer changes me. God also gives prayer to me as a way to cry out to Him with sadness, grief, and sorrow over the situations I face. I love to see how David did this so many times in the Psalms.

Prayer can and should include these things:

- Praise to God
- Thanksgiving for all the blessings I have received from Him
- Confession of all known sin every day
- Praying for myself to grow in Christ
- Praying for others

These things help to widen my perspective and keep my eyes on my Lord, who is outside time and space. It helps me look past my current little snapshot in time and my little world.

SCRIPTURE GROUNDS US IN KNOWLEDGE

I also desperately need lots of time to feast on God's Word, to digest His truth and love, to sit at His feet, to get to know Him more, to listen to His voice, to absorb His goodness, and to allow Him to restore my soul. If prayer is my communication with God, Scripture is one of the strongest ways God speaks to us. There's a reason we call it the Word of God. Taking time to learn from God's words spoken through the heroes of our faith can help lift our eyes toward heaven, tell us what to expect, and encourage us to pursue God.

In addition, I can't pray powerfully in God's Spirit if I am depleted.

Scripture gives encouragement, rebuke, insight—in short, it fills me up. It gives me the ability to grow in my faith and to reach greater heights of spiritual maturity, wisdom, and insight. As a mom, I need all the spiritual maturity and growth I can get, because I want to be able to live out the most godly example to my children as Jesus's power flows through me.

A Life of Thanksgiving and a Heart of Praise

What better way to keep my eyes on eternal, heavenly things than to fill my mind and heart with all the things I can be thankful for in Christ and to fill my mouth with His praises? Satan hates to be around my praises to God. God loves to hear my praises and all my grateful thoughts toward Him. Sometimes it is challenging to get myself to verbalize thankfulness and praises for God. But it helps if I just make talking about things I am thankful for a routine part of my day.

In the afternoon, on the way home from school, I like to ask my children, "What are some things you are really thankful for today?" I also like to ask them, "What are some of God's qualities that you admire greatly and would like to praise?" Sometimes, we may sing praise songs together. There is so much power in worshiping in song together as a family! Other times, I may invite my children to pray out loud and to praise and thank God for things that come to their minds. They don't even have to close their eyes. I always like to thank Him for things as I go about my day.

Toiletries	Worship music
Clean, running water	God's wisdom for us
Electricity	Marriage/family
Internet	Our relationships
Our cars, home, and jobs	Nutritious, delicious food
Our government	Physical and spiritual rest
Freedom to worship God	Stores

Working roads

Our church and church
  leaders

Creation

Sunrises and sunsets

Seasons

Our senses

The Bible

God's sovereignty

God's character

Answered prayers (yes, wait,
  and no)

Miracles I have seen

Testimonies of faithful
  believers

Trials

What a blessing to focus on God's provision and to remind myself and my children of His presence and that all that we have comes from Him. God is our Provider. He is the one who ensures we have a supply of food, clean water, and clean air. He provides for what we need today in this physical life. He will provide for our needs in heaven forever.

As I focus on gratitude and praise, I set my heart on things that are eternally significant and things that please the Lord. It is difficult to harbor doubt, fear, and worry while I am praising and thanking God, remembering all He has done for His people in the past and for my family and me. My trust and faith in Him boost my ability to see the things that truly matter beyond this moment and help me keep proper perspective as I relate to and love my children. My ability to see with an eternal perspective leads to peace for me as a mom and helps me lead my children to peace in the Lord as well.

A Peaceful Mom's Prayer

Lord,

I pray that You might give me Your vision, Your perspective, and Your heart as I seek to raise my precious children to know and love You. Help me to remember what is truly most impor-tant in Your sight. Help me to align my priorities with Your own. Correct me when I stray off course. Let me love what You love and hate what You hate. Empower me to store up treasures in heaven. Help me keep my eyes on You and on heavenly things so I can be the mom You desire me to be for these children You have so graciously entrusted to my care.

Amen.

Avoiding Some Common Mistakes

But God demonstrates his own love for us in this: While we were still sinners, Christ died for us. (Romans 5:8)

The standard of love God desires me to show to all other people, including my children, is His own love for us. I love them because God loves them and God loves me. I allow God's unconditional love to pour through me into my children's lives. I like to think of my life as a pipe. I want it to be as cleaned out as possible on the inside to allow God's Spirit and His goodness and love to blast through me. Then His love can saturate everyone around me.

Without reservation, I want to do what is best for my children in God's sight, knowing I am accountable to God for the way I parent, teach, discipline, and love my children. I am His representative to demonstrate divine love to them. They learn how to relate to other people by my example. They learn what God's love is and who God is by the way I love them. I love them because they are my children and because they are made in the image of God—no matter what they may do.

The world's love is all about me. It is selfish and uses manipulation to get what it wants for itself. The love God commands me to show to others is the same kind of love God shows me. It is sacrificial, humble, and faithful. It is not selfish. It is not self-seeking. It does not manipulate. It is not fake. It is genuine, deep, unfailing love that seeks first to please Christ and then to bless my children even if it costs me. (The best description of God's love is found in 1 Corinthians 13:4–8).

I will make mistakes and stumble into sin as a parent at times. Hopefully, when I fall short, I will quickly get back up with God's help and set a better example. But sometimes it may take years before I see certain sins I may have committed against my children. No one had completely perfect examples for parents. No one is completely perfect on this side of heaven. I want to be open to the ways God may desire me to grow and mature in how I relate to others, especially my family.

> "The love God commands me
> to show to others is the same
> kind of love God shows me."

For some of us, the common mistakes or sins we will discuss later in this chapter just feel like "normal" family relationships. But the fact is, "normal" in this world isn't what God desires for us. He wants to give us infinitely more than we can imagine (Eph. 3:20). Jesus came to restore our relationship with God to the "pre-fall" state. He wants to restore our relationships with people to that same healthy state as well. As we allow His Spirit to have control, we can have victory over these issues in real life.

Let's take some time to look at the real motives behind our not-so-perfect approaches and why they are not honoring to God or healthy for our children. Then we'll find the better way God has for our families.

What causes fights and quarrels among you? Don't they come from your desires that battle within you? You desire but do not have, so you kill. You covet but you cannot get what you want, so you quarrel and fight. You do not have because you do not ask God. When you ask, you do not receive, because you ask with wrong motives, that you may spend what you get on your pleasures. (James 4:1–3)

LOVING WITH STRINGS ATTACHED

I'll love you *if* . . . This is manipulation. It is a business transaction, not an unconditional relationship. It's the way the world loves: "If you give me what I want from you, then I will give you what you want from me." Or, "I'll love you if you love me." This is not the way God loves. Children see through this kind of "love" for what it is, and as they get older, they will pull away because they will tire of performing for me. They know it isn't love.

Manipulation repels our children and encourages them to resent us. God calls me to love because His Spirit creates a heart of love in me and that is my new character in Christ. It is not about me getting something out of the deal from another person. My job is simply to love, not to fish for "What's in this for me?"

> If you love those who love you, what credit is that to you? Even sinners love those who love them. And if you do good to those who are good to you, what credit is that to you? Even sinners do that. . . . But love your enemies, do good to them, and lend to them without expecting to get anything back. Then your reward will be great, and you will be children of the Most High, because he is kind to the ungrateful and wicked. Be merciful, just as your Father is merciful. (Luke 6:32–36)

A Gift Is Not Really a Gift If There Are Strings

Imagine I gave my daughter a gift for her birthday that she loved—perhaps a beautiful doll. A healthy way to give gifts is to give them simply out of love, with the giver expecting no specific behavior in return.

But what if I give a gift to my daughter and then my daughter misbehaves? Imagine that I say something like, "I'm going to take that gift back that I gave you if you act like this." If I do that, I just taught my daughter that she does not receive gifts because she is loved but because she earned them—and she must keep earning them indefinitely.

It is good for me to give consequences for misbehavior. It is even fine to take a toy for a time in an act of loving discipline. But, in my view, a more healthy approach would be, "Honey, because you disobeyed Mama, you have lost your favorite toy for the rest of the day. You may have it back tomorrow. Please obey Mama next time. If you disobey one of your parents, you won't be able to play with your doll that day."

This way I am giving appropriate discipline and correction. I am addressing her disobedience. But I am not attaching strings to my love or to my gifts. There is a critical difference in those approaches. The strings-attached approach leads to a child feeling shame, inappropriate guilt, and betrayal. The second approach would encourage a child to take personal responsibility for obedience because she wants to avoid negative consequences. But she knows that my love for her and my gifts to her are not on the line. Those things are always hers to keep.

Helping with Strings Attached

Another way I might love with strings attached would be that I do something for my son, such as helping him with his applications to college. Then he makes a decision I don't agree with, but it is his personal decision to make—for instance, he decides to go to college two hours away, and he has a full scholarship to cover the cost. In this example, let's say that this particular son has shown great responsibility and trustworthiness. So I don't have concerns that he is planning to use his freedom irresponsibly. This is his dream, and it is time for him to begin to spread his wings and fly a bit on his own.

Imagine that I say with bitterness, "After I did so much for you all these years and with your college applications—*this* is how you repay me? You just leave me like this? You know I wanted you to go to the university ten minutes away from here so you could be home with me. Now I'll be completely alone and miserable, and it's all your fault! You know I can't be happy if you're not here. How could you do this to me!"

I expect him to stay in town because of my "generosity" to him, and I am trying to make him responsible for my emotional well-being. There are a lot of expectations attached to the things I do for him in this scenario. If my children don't meet my expectations later, I use the things I gave them to try to blackmail them into doing my will. If they refuse to do what I want, I will seethe with resentment and may attempt to put them on guilt trips to try to continue to make them do things my way. I will cripple my relationships with my children and erode their trust in me if this is my approach.

What are the signs that I may be loving with strings attached? I may not even realize I love my children conditionally. Sometimes it is helpful to see some black-and-white examples so I can evaluate my approach. (Note—loving conditionally is different from giving proper consequences and discipline to our children when they misbehave.) Here are some things I might say or do that reveal I have conditions attached to my love:

- My love is like a business transaction: "If you do this for me, then I will love you. If you don't do what I want, I will take away my love."
- I try to bribe my children to love me.
- I love my children in order to get what I want.
- My motives, if I examine them closely, are what I think is best for me.
- If my children don't perform to my satisfaction, I punish them emotionally.
- I try to crush their spirits if they don't do what I want them to do.

- I am not prioritizing what is ultimately best for my children.
- I use my love or my withdrawal of love, rather than natural consequences, as a reward and punishment for behavior.
- I say things like, "You don't love me. If you loved me, you would . . ."
- I am willing to even disown my children to punish them as they get older, if they don't do what I want them to do.

How Could I Show Healthy Love as a Peaceful Mom?

My love is not supposed to be a reward or punishment. Consequences are supposed to serve as rewards or punishments—especially "natural consequences" that make sense based on whatever my child did that was wrong. Consequences have nothing to do with my love for my children, other than the fact that I discipline them from a heart of love, not from anger or hatred. My love, as a parent, is supposed to be constant and unconditional like God's love (1 Cor. 13:4–8).

I will have to give different consequences to my children depending on their obedience or disobedience, but my love should stay the same, even when I am grieved by their choices. Love is not supposed to be a business transaction, either. It should be freely given because love is my nature as a Christian mom. My children should be able to feel secure in my love, knowing I will always be there for them and always seek to do what is ultimately in their best interests.

Here are some ways I might try to approach my children—peaceful mom style:

- "I will love you no matter what you choose. If you decide to go to college two hours away, I will miss you so much. But I will always love and support you. I want what is best for you."
- "This gift is yours just for being you. I love you and want to give you this as a way to show you my love."
- "Because you didn't take out the trash like I asked you to last

night and the garbage truck already came by, please put the trash in your truck and take it to the dump today."

- "I'm very disappointed that you have decided to make such an unwise decision. But I still love you. Let's work through this together. I want to see you make better choices. Because of your disobedience, you will not be able to have friends over for a week. And you will have to re-earn my trust. Here is what we need to do to get back on track . . . Let's pray together about this. We are on the same team here."
- "I want what is best for you and what God wants for you. Even if it is hard on me."
- "I want you to know that you are precious to me. Your thoughts, ideas, feelings, and concerns matter, even if we don't agree. I want you to feel heard."
- "I'd love for you to try this extracurricular activity, but if this one doesn't interest you, let's look into one that does."

ATTEMPTING TO CONTROL OTHERS

If I don't trust the Holy Spirit to do His job and I don't honor my children's free will, I may feel compelled to try to force my children to do what I think they should do. Shame and guilt are powerful negative motivators that the flesh loves to use. I might think I am winning a few battles because they may cave in and do what I want in order to avoid conflict with me for a while. But if I try to force my children to do things my way, I may ultimately hurt them and my relationship with them.

I must remember that I am not God. I get to make my choices and have my own thoughts. My children get to make their own choices and have their own thoughts. I don't get to control their thoughts. God can open people's hearts to conviction and repentance, but I can't. And truly, even though God could force people to do things, He doesn't. He is a gentleman, and He gives us all free will. If God Himself doesn't wrestle people's decisions from them, that may be a good indication to me that it is unwise for me to try to do that, too.

> Godly sorrow brings repentance that leads to salvation and leaves no regret, but worldly sorrow brings death. (2 Cor. 7:10)

> When [the Holy Spirit] comes, he will prove the world to be in the wrong about sin and righteousness and judgment. (John 16:8)

The problem is, when I try to control others, I destroy emotional intimacy and trust. My children will likely rebel against me trying to force them into specific decisions when the choices are truly theirs to make. No one wants to feel smothered. I will have more control when my children are very young than I should have when they are older. There should be a process of giving them more responsibilities and greater independence as they grow and mature. This requires discernment and godly wisdom.

"When I try to control others, I destroy emotional intimacy and trust."

But even younger children can think for themselves. I can't make them agree with me. I can discipline, correct them, and instruct them. For example, I can make my five-year-old daughter apologize if she mistreated her brother, but I can't change her heart and her thinking. I can teach her God's ways. I can show her the right way to think. I can live out a godly example in front of her. But even then, she has free will; it is her choice whether or not she will receive the instruction and apply it.

I can rightly seek to influence my children's decisions and pray for them with pure motives even as they get older. But I don't get to make every decision for them or coerce them into specific decisions. The number of decisions I can rightfully make for my children will decrease over time, until eventually, they will make all their decisions themselves.

Many of the same things that feel disrespectful to my husband also hurt my children—and other people as well. Honestly, we all want to feel valued, loved, safe, cherished, and respected—husbands, wives, and children.

Here are some possible ways I might try to control those I love:

Shame, blame, or guilt
- "You always ruin everything."
- "A decent son would be happy to do this for his mom."
- "If only I had a daughter who really cared about me."
- "How could you do this to me?"

Insults, name-calling, cursing, threats
- "You are such an idiot!"
- "If you don't do X, I will make your life miserable."
- "If you date this awful girl, I will tell her all your darkest secrets so she'll never want to be with you again, and there is nothing you can do to stop me."

Verbal pressure and demands, often with an angry, harsh tone of voice or yelling
- "I said do it right now! Do you hear me? Get up!"
- "Do exactly what I said, and you better have it done in thirty seconds or less, or else!"

Financial pressure or sabotage

Humiliation

Fear of my disapproval

Flattery and insincere compliments

Bribery with rewards and special treats

Gossiping to others when a person resists me

Trying to get other people to pressure my child for me

Here are some signs that I may have significant issues with control as a mom and wife:

- I do not admit fault.
- I do not genuinely apologize or take real responsibility for my sin but blame others for my wrong behavior.
- Everything has to be my way.
- I subconsciously or consciously expect others and even God to submit to me.
- I am inflexible.
- I struggle with unforgiveness.
- I believe I don't have much sin in my life.
- I believe I am almost always right.
- I think I know what's best for others.
- I can't receive the wisdom or different perspectives others may want to share with me.
- I think everyone should think exactly like I do, or they must be wrong.
- I think I am the only one who can discern God's will.
- I believe that my wisdom is genuinely much greater than that of everyone else.
- I want others to fear my wrath if they don't do things my way.
- I try to lord power over other people to force them to do what I want.
- I want others to desire my approval more than anything.
- I get highly offended if anyone dares to question me or disagree with me.
- I expect others to be responsible for my emotions, decisions, and happiness.
- I try to be responsible for others' emotions, decisions, and happiness.
- I have a critical, judgmental spirit.

- I think I am helping, but others don't seem to appreciate all my help, advice, and wisdom.
- I'm very afraid and anxious if I feel I don't have control; my world will fall apart.

WHAT MY TEENAGE SON REALLY NEEDED —JACOB'S STORY

"Teenage sons respond well to respect rather than control." This resonates strongly with me. This was a particular problem for my wife and my youngest son when he was thirteen or fourteen. She was consistently having trouble controlling him and would frequently seek my intervention (and then complain about whatever approach I took with him to get whatever compliance she wanted from him).

One time that I'll always remember, she was completely frustrated with him and came into my home office to demand my intervention. She had been demanding something from him, raising her voice, and treating him pretty contemptuously (a mode she frequently used for me as well).

For some reason, I recognized as soon as he came into my office that he was not just defiant but sad. Somehow I knew that coming on strong was just going to make things worse, so instead I went over to where he was sitting and just gave him a big hug (this was not my normal way to begin a disciplinary session); after a few moments, he just slumped into me, and when I asked him what was wrong, he broke into tears and began to explain what he was feeling and what was bothering him. When he was done, he readily agreed to do whatever it was his mother had been trying to get him to do.

How Could I Love Without Control as a Peaceful Mom?

It may be tempting to overcorrect a controlling tendency by becoming totally passive. I probably will overshoot a bit one way and then the other as I ask God to help me overcome my control addiction. But the goal is not to be passive. It is to be in a place of delicate balance where I am not bossy, condescending, and trying to take on God's sovereignty, but I am still taking responsibility for myself and being a good steward of the position God has given me for His glory.

Of course, exactly how I love without controlling will vary a bit depending on my children's ages and personalities. I want to be more flexible and do less "telling them what to do" as they get older. Younger children need more instruction and supervision, but older children will begin to feel smothered if I hover over them too much. I want to have a pleasant tone of voice, friendly facial expression, and use good manners when speaking to my children.

Here are some ways I may want to try loving my children without controlling them as a peaceful mom:

- "I'd love to hear your ideas about what you'd like to do tonight as a family."
- "That's a great suggestion. Let's try it your way this time."
- "Would you mind explaining a bit more about the way you look at this situation? I've never heard this perspective before and would like to understand your thoughts better."
- "I'm feeling really sad right now, and I wish we could spend more time together."
- "Would you like to wear this outfit or that one?" (Try this with young children who can't appropriately choose their clothing yet.)
- "You can wear whatever you think is best, as long as it comes at least to your [fingertips, knees, or whatever the standard is in your family]." (Try this with older children who are choosing their own clothing.)

- "Wow, you are going to have ketchup on your waffle? I don't think I would enjoy that. But maybe you'll like it. It could be a good idea not to cover the whole waffle with ketchup just in case you don't like it."
- "What do you think would help you concentrate better when you are doing your homework?"
- "Would you please do this chore now? Thanks so much!"

When I am not trying to control other people, I have more peace and they have more peace, too. A peaceful mom knows she doesn't have to try to force everything to go a certain way all the time. I can humbly acknowledge that other people have wisdom to share and important perspectives, too. I am able to roll with things in a flexible way. I have authority as a mom that my children don't have. But I don't have to be a dictator. I can be benevolent, reasonable, approachable, respectful, and loving.

Playing the Martyr

Merriam-Webster defines "playing the martyr" as "to act like someone who deserves admiration or sympathy because of being badly treated."[5] When I "play the martyr," I insist on doing something I clearly don't want to do so I can hold it over the heads of those I "help." Usually it is a chore or some act of service that I do for my family.

Then I may try to make my family feel guilty about what I did for them to get them to do what I want later. This is not godly love—it is manipulation. It puts my loved ones in a position that is lose-lose. I give love and serve my children with bitterness and resentment.

When a mother plays the martyr, she puts her family in a terrible catch-22. They either have to blatantly disrespect her and go against what she says she wants so they can help her with the chores that seem to be such a burden to her, or they have to try to respect her words, only to suffer later by hearing her complain about how no one would help her—which wasn't even true. When a mother employs this technique, she repels her husband and children. This approach creates great frustration and resentment for family members.

> "When a mother plays the martyr, she
> puts her family in a terrible catch-22."

Often, they eventually just leave her to her chores and complaining because they don't know what else to do. She is upset when they help and upset when they don't help. So eventually they conclude, "Why bother trying to help? She seems intent on being miserable and being angry with us no matter what." How can they love a woman who doesn't want to enjoy anything with them, who seems to only want to bitterly complain about how terrible they all are, and who won't receive their help? Then when her children make plans with friends to go somewhere else as often as possible, Mom laments that no one ever wants to be with her, saying, "Obviously, you don't love me as much as I love you!"

Trash Night with a Martyr Mom

Imagine that a mom resents taking out the trash every week. She complains about it every time she has to do it. Her teenage son and daughter offer to do it. But she says, "No, no. You'll do it wrong. You don't tie the handles right, and everything will spill out and make a big mess that I will end up having to clean up. I'll just have to do it myself, the way I have to do everything around here."

Her husband comes in and suggests going for a walk together. The mom says, "Oh, you all go on without me. I have to get the trash together since no one will help me. I don't have time for fun like all of you do."

Her husband offers to carry the trash out so she can come, but the mom gets upset at him. He decides to respect her wishes and let her handle the trash by herself and lets her miss out on the family fun time together. After the family returns from the walk, they find Mom lying on the couch with an ice pack on her shoulder. She spews anger at them.

"Shouldn't you all be ashamed of yourselves?" she says. "Going on a walk when I obviously needed help? I pulled my shoulder trying to throw that heavy trash bag in the trash bin outside. I knew I shouldn't have tried to carry the trash out myself. I knew it was too heavy. But did any of you care? No! Now I'm going to be hurting for weeks because no one would help me. Fine family I have! And now I am going to get behind on all the laundry and the vacuuming, too. But don't any of you touch anything because you'll just ruin the laundry and none of you know how to run the vacuum without messing it up!"

My characteristics when I am "playing the martyr" are things such as grumpiness, irritability, resentment, bitterness, complaining, arguing, and hostility. If I do all the chores in the house, but don't have love for my family, what does 1 Corinthians 13:1–3 say? If I do great things without love—I am just making useless noise. I am nothing. I gain nothing.

Here are some signs I am playing the martyr:

- I resent doing things for my children, and I let them know about it.
- If I ask them for help, I won't let them help me, and then I feel angry with them for not helping me.
- I feel that "I have to do everything."
- I thrive on feeling extremely needed and indispensable, especially when it comes to chores around the house.
- I may equate cooking and doing chores with loving others.
- I blame others for my misery.
- I like for others to pity me.
- I want people to admire me for my suffering.
- I won't ask for what I need or share my needs and concerns simply and vulnerably.
- I won't receive help or love from others.

- I believe that if people love me, they should just know what I need and do it.

How Could I Request Help as a Peaceful Mom?

Thankfully, there is a better way! I can ask for what I need vulnerably and respectfully. I can receive help from others even if they do things differently from how I do them. I can then join my family in doing fun things together. I can change the emotional thermostat from "cold and hostile" to "warm and inviting." I can focus on growing in my ability to love with God's love and to be a blessing to my family.

Imagine a mom saying these kinds of things with a pleasant tone of voice and a genuine, friendly smile:

- "Hey, would you please help me take out the trash tonight? That would be great!"
- "Oops, I think some trash spilled. Would you please clean that up? Thanks so much!"
- "I appreciate everyone's help. We make a great team."
- "I'm so glad you are my children. You are such a blessing to me!"
- "Thanks for helping me with the chores so I can go on the walk, too. I wouldn't miss this time together with my family for the world!"
- "Let's think about things we are thankful for today. I'll start!"
- "I'd love to teach the kids how to sort the laundry and how to hang Dad's shirts. That will free me up so we can play some family games more often in the evenings."

DIVISIVENESS

Merriam-Webster defines *divisiveness* as "creating disunity or dissension."[6] All it takes is my having a conversation with one child about another family member and painting that other family member in a negative light. "I'm so glad you aren't like your brother. He is so lazy sometimes. You have such a strong work ethic. He should be more like you."

If I say something like this to my daughter, what is she going to be thinking? Negative things about her brother, of course. She may even decide to insult him to his face because I just encouraged her to think that way. Just a few negative, judgmental words and a critical spirit about the others in the family go a long way to destroying unity, peace, and love.

After a divisive comment like this, there is a tendency for other family members to either rally toward or against the one I criticized underhandedly, which creates factions.

> Warn a divisive person once, and then warn them a second time. After that, have nothing to do with them. You may be sure that such people are warped and sinful; they are self-condemned. (Titus 3:10–11)

This is a favorite tool of the enemy. If he can get me to unwittingly try to promote hatred, resentment, and hurt feelings, he can accomplish many of his purposes in my family. Often, divisiveness involves talking about others "behind their backs" to try to incite anger, jealousy, self-righteousness, or resentment. If I am being divisive, I might try to make people think I am on "their side" and then tell them how someone else in the family is "against them." The goal is to try to alienate people and create tension. Of course, most of us don't realize that is what we are doing at the time.

There are countless ways I could encourage disunity. Whether I am being divisive on purpose or unintentionally, the results are the same.

Here are some ways I might contribute to division in my family:

- I try to persuade one family member to have negative feelings toward another.

- I spread lies about someone in the family to try to hurt them.
- I show favoritism to one child over another.
- I treat my children unfairly, giving more chores or more punishment to certain ones.
- I ignore my husband, cultivating resentment of the attention I give to our children.
- I say hateful things about my children to them or to each other.
- I involve extended family and spread the hurt feelings even further.
- I show favoritism to my children's friends over my children.
- I make negative assumptions about one family member and articulate them to others to help create doubt about someone else's character and motives.
- I accuse people of wrong motives without knowing the truth or understanding their perspectives.

How Could I Approach Our Differences as a Peaceful Mom?

As a mom who values healthy communication and relationships, I want to treat all my children equally. I want them to know that I love each of them very much and to the same degree. I want to promote unity, godly thoughts, and unconditional love.

I can do this with practices like these:

- I counter negative feelings someone may have about someone else with positive things.
- I encourage my children not to complain or argue and model these things myself.
- I try to handle discipline fairly without any bias or favoritism.
- I say positive things about my children and husband in front of everyone.
- I keep emotional "dirty laundry" out of sight of extended family whenever possible.
- I treat my children and their friends fairly.

- I avoid making negative assumptions but rather articulate positive assumptions to my family members, helping them to assume the best of others.
- I seek to understand others before making accusations.

My words have so much influence and power in my family to either build others up or tear them down. I need God's help to restrain my mouth and my words before I speak rashly. Proverbs 10:19 says, "When there are many words, sin is unavoidable, but the one who controls his lips is wise" (HCSB).

How I used to hate that verse! I like to talk a lot. For many years, I couldn't see that my talking involved any sin at all. But then God opened my eyes. Wow. At first, I felt like it would be best for me never to talk again. Almost every word out of my mouth was the result of some kind of sinful motive. How desperately I needed the Holy Spirit to completely take over my tongue!

Loose Lips

James tells us that the tongue, though small, is extremely powerful—the spark that starts an entire forest on fire (James 3:5). If we aren't careful to control our tongues, we can destroy our families.

Oversharing is very easy to do as a mom. When my children are babies, I can share absolutely everything they do with other people, and it doesn't hurt my kids' feelings. Of course, at that age, they also don't know the difference yet between right and wrong, so they aren't purposely making wrong choices or having internal struggles. I may get used to sharing entertaining little stories about my young children with extended family, friends, and on social media.

However, as my children grow, they would appreciate more discernment from me about the things I share. Otherwise, I will lose their trust and they will feel betrayed. What I share may not even be bad or negative in my estimation, but if my children are hurt by what

I share with others, I want to stop and rethink what things I should tell others.

Here are some ways I could overshare about my children:

- "Brenden was so upset about not making the middle school basketball team. The poor boy cried for hours about it."
- "Lucy had a bedwetting accident again! She's seven years old. Why can't she get this under control?"
- "Eric really hates it when I share this story from when he was little, but it is just so funny! Let me tell you what happened . . ."
- "Nate doesn't have any friends at high school. It's so sad."
- "Jill just started her period last week. Can you believe it?"

In some situations, some of these things above may be appropriate for me to share. But I will need the discernment of God's Spirit to help me decide when it may be best not to share.

Gossip is a bit different from oversharing but even more harmful. Generally, when I gossip, it is to try to make myself look better or more important than someone else. It is often to try to get people to think less of the person I am talking about and more of me. The root of gossip is usually pride, self-righteousness, jealousy, or resentment. Oversharing and gossip are often key ingredients in creating division, resentment, and even hatred in our families.

> "Even if I don't purposely intend to hurt others, gossip leads to hurt feelings, division, and bitterness."

Even if I don't purposely intend to hurt others, gossip leads to hurt feelings, division, and bitterness. It can destroy individuals, families, businesses, churches, and even governments. It's easy to think of gossip as being "a little sin," but in reality, the consequences can be catastrophic.

A perverse person stirs up conflict,
　　and a gossip separates close friends. (Prov. 16:28)

Do not let any unwholesome talk come out of your mouths, but
only what is helpful for building others up according to their
needs, that it may benefit those who listen. (Eph. 4:29)

Those who consider themselves religious and yet do not keep a
tight rein on their tongues deceive themselves, and their reli-
gion is worthless. (James 1:26)

Here are some ways I could gossip about my children:

- "Katie has a crush on a boy in her middle school class. She told me
  not to tell anyone, but it is just so cute, I had to share it with you!"
- "Hank's friend got into big trouble at school this week. Don't tell
  anyone else, but he cheated on a test and now he is suspended."
- "Taylor has such a bad habit of looking at porn online. I can't
  believe she got into that stuff. What was she thinking!"
- "Emma is so sensitive about her weight. She could really stand to
  lose about twenty pounds, but she pitches a fit if I mention anything about it."

Insults also hurt my children. A mom has a unique position of power
and influence to shape a child's future inner voice. Her praise shapes
and inspires her children for a lifetime. Her insults resonate more
deeply and more painfully than anything the bully at school could ever
say. What I say to my children to encourage them or to discipline them
stays with them.

I have met grown men and women who still believe every negative
word their mothers said to them. They have embraced the toxic words
as their identity, and now, even if their mothers are no longer alive,

those words continue to live on every day as the grown child's inner dialogue. I have also met adults whose mothers poured life-giving words into their lives, and that has become their inner dialogue. What a blessing!

We can allow the enemy of our souls to pour through our speech into our children to speak death to them, or we can allow the Holy Spirit of God to pour through our speech and into our children to speak life to them.

Here are some ways I could speak "death" to my child:

- "You will never amount to anything."
- "You are worthless."
- "I wish you were a girl. Men are all dogs."
- "I wish you were a boy. Girls are such a pain."
- "Marriage is slavery. Don't ever get married. You'll totally regret it."
- "Children are a huge burden."
- "No one will ever want to marry you."
- "If you don't lose weight, you'll never get a boyfriend."
- "You are ugly."
- "You are stupid."
- "I hate you."
- "I wish you were never born."
- "You are such a waste of my time."
- "Just a minute" (not occasionally, but constantly).
- "Will you be quiet for once!"
- "Why are you always . . . ?"
- "Why can't you be like your [brother or sister]?"
- "You are always . . . !"
- "You never get things right!"
- "You are a lazy slob."
- "Why did I think I wanted to have children?"
- "I hope you have a child this horrible one day."

Here are some ways I could speak life to my child:

- "I love you and will be here for you no matter what."
- "I believe in you."
- "I can't wait to see the good plans God has in store for you and how He wants to use you for His kingdom."
- "You are precious."
- "Men and women are both so important in the world and in families."
- "Children are a wonderful blessing from God."
- "I'm praying for a godly spouse for you if it is God's will."
- "You have value because God created you and because He loves you so much!"
- "Look at the ways God has gifted you."
- "I love you more than I could ever explain to you."
- "I'm so glad God gave you to us. You are a joy and a blessing."

How Could I Approach My Words as a Peaceful Mom?

There is a reason for the saying "loose lips sink ships." I want to be careful about what I share:

- On Facebook and social media (something that is cute when my children are little may be embarrassing to them later)
- With my children's friends, or later with their boyfriends or girl-friends
- With my children's teachers or bosses
- With people in my circle of influence
- With prayer partners
- With my coworkers
- With extended family
- Even with my husband, to a degree
- With my children

I want to stop and evaluate the price my child will pay if I share certain stories. Sometimes I may convince myself that certain things are okay to share because they are "prayer requests." But even then, I need to use wisdom, discernment, and respect for my children concerning what I share and how much detail I share. I want to keep their trust in me intact. I don't want to share things that will hurt them or create regret later. If I know my child would be upset if I shared something with someone, it is probably wise not to share it. If I am not sure, it may be best if I ask permission from my child before I say anything to anyone else.

Here are some litmus tests to help me decide if I should spread specific information about my children:

- Am I about to share negative or embarrassing things?
- What are my motives? (Am I just trying to entertain other people? Am I trying to hurt my children or make people think less of them? Am I trying to make myself look better?)
- Could I say what I am about to say with my child there and be confident that he would be okay with it?
- Am I about to say something that my child asked me to keep in confidence?
- Would my child feel disrespected by me or betrayed if I talk about this story?
- Am I speaking only to a godly mentor for wisdom about a difficult situation, or am I tempted to spread something negative to many people?

Here are some ways to check my approach about what I say to my children:

- Am I seeking to build them up in love and truth or hurt them?
- Will these words speak death or God's life to them?

- Do I want them to remember these words and say them to themselves for many years to come?
- Am I supporting God's Word and His truth about my child's identity in what I want to say?
- Do I have a critical spirit, bitterness, sinful anger, hatred, unforgiveness, legalism, or any other sinful motives in my heart that I need to address first?

PROJECTING A POOR BODY IMAGE

As a Christian wife and mother, part of my job is to project godly femininity and to live it out before my children in a healthy way for them to observe and imitate. I am an identical twin, so I know the pain of being constantly compared to someone else in every single way. Other people compared us to each other, and we compared ourselves, too. You never want to be the ugly twin, the fat twin, the stupid twin, and so forth. What a destructive way to live—constantly comparing myself to someone else.

It is enough to be myself. My new self in Christ, that is! It is enough to be who God made me to be. It is enough that God loves me and I am His. My children—my son and daughter—need to see this message in my life. When I belong to Christ, I am free from this world and its ways of thinking. I don't have to be a slave to fashion, to the beauty industry, to worldly ideas about beauty, or to the comparing game anymore!

I don't have to reveal my body to everyone to feel like I am "attractive and beautiful enough." I can show respect for myself, for my sexuality, for God, and for others by dressing modestly. I don't have to try to win the approval of other people. Of course, I wouldn't purposely try to embarrass my husband or children with my appearance. But I don't have to be desperate for other people's approval of my appearance. I can teach my children to embrace the same mind-set that is grounded in God's Word rather than in man's word.

God loves variety. Every flower is beautiful to Him. Every creature brings Him delight and glory. Every person is precious and beautiful to Him. I don't have to look a certain way for Him to accept me. My worth does not come from any of these things that seem to matter so much in our world.

Instead of focusing primarily on worldly beauty—I can think and teach my children things such as these.

Biblical Truths About Body Image

Healthy Thought	Bible References
I thank God for the way He made me.	I am fearfully and wonderfully made. (Ps. 139:14)
I accept the way He made me, and what He made is good.	God saw all that he had made, and it was very good. (Gen. 1:31)
I am content with the body God gave me.	Godliness with contentment is great gain. (1 Tim. 6:6)
I am confident in my skin because God made me and He gives me my value.	I am made in the image of God. (Gen. 1:27)
I am confident in His love and will rest in God's love and peace.	Now we who have believed enter that rest. (Heb. 4:3)
I long for the radiant, heavenly inner beauty that delights God.	The unfading beauty of a gentle and quiet spirit, which is of great worth in God's sight . . . do what is right and do not give way to fear. (1 Peter 3:4, 6)
When I feel insecure, I will look to the cross and remember the Love that came from heaven to rescue me and claim me for Himself.	For God so loved [my name] that he gave his one and only Son, that [if I believe] in him [I] shall not perish but have eternal life. (John 3:16)

Healthy Thought	Bible References
It's okay that there are women in the world who are more physically beautiful than I am—I don't have to compete with anyone.	I have learned to be content whatever the circumstances [whether I am the most physically beautiful or the least physically beautiful woman in the room] through Christ who gives me strength. (Phil. 4:12–13)
My value doesn't come from my external beauty. It comes from my relationship with Jesus and the beauty He is creating in my heart, mind, and soul.	Charm is deceptive, and beauty is fleeting; but a woman who fears the LORD is to be praised. (Prov. 31:30)
I may put some effort into looking my best at times, but I am not going to make outer beauty or thinness or any worldly thing into the most important thing or one of the top things in my life.	For since there is jealousy and quarreling among you, are you not worldly? Are you not acting like mere humans? (1 Cor. 3:3)
My hope and contentment are in Christ alone.	Be content with what you have, because God has said, "Never will I leave you; never will I forsake you." (Heb. 13:5)

A Peaceful Mom's Prayer

Lord,

Your wisdom is so much higher than my own. Help me to evaluate my thoughts and motives correctly in the light of Your Word. Help me to discern truth from lies. Let me clearly see Your way, and give me the desire and strength to always choose rightly. I may not have had perfect examples as I was growing up, but now You are my Father, and You are my perfect example. I lay aside my worldly, human wisdom, and seek to do things Your way. Let my life speak life to my children. Make me healthy in Your sight that I might model a godly example to them, to help them learn healthy ways to love and to relate to people.

Amen.

Counting Trials as Joy

Consider it pure joy, my brothers and sisters, whenever you
face trials of many kinds. (James 1:2)

Imagine that your nine-year-old daughter is at church camp for the first time when you get a call at eleven o'clock Monday night. The camp director apologizes for calling so late, but she wanted to let you know that your daughter fell out of her top bunk and hit her head. She seems confused and has vomited a few times. The director would like your permission to transport your daughter to the nearest hospital, which is a two-hour drive from your house. How do you react to this trial?

Or imagine that your eleven-year-old son declares that he doesn't want to go to school anymore. Some of the other boys were bullying him, and he is not taking it well at all. He is so upset that he barely eats for days and complains of a stomachache constantly. How do you react to this trial?

As a mom, my first instinct is to want to make every problem go away and fix my child's pain instantly. I can absolutely hug, love, encourage, and comfort my children. I can want to fix the problems as much as I can. But I can also be an instrument God uses to help point them to much greater things that God may want to accomplish.

God can and will use the small and big trials we face to mature us, to strengthen our faith, to help us grow much stronger spiritually as we trust Him to do these things in our lives. This is an ironclad promise to those who belong to Him. He can even use our trials and suffering for His glory. It is often only in the difficult times, when our faith is challenged, that we really do grow. When I know a bit about the good things that God can bring from painful times, it helps me to look past the painful trial to the joy that awaits me. When I can see with an eternal perspective like this, I can even learn to experience God's joy during the trial.

Imagine if I teach my children to embrace the pruning shears of God with patience and anticipation, rejoicing in the good He is doing even before we can see the good results. What a priceless gift! If I know how to look for the good and beauty in hardships and I can identify that I am going through a refining fire of the Lord to make me stronger, what peace I can experience in my heart, even in the midst of a significant roadblock!

> Endure hardship as discipline; God is treating you as his children. For what children are not disciplined by their father? . . . They disciplined us for a little while as they thought best; but God disciplines us for our good, in order that we may share in his holiness. No discipline seems pleasant at the time, but painful. Later on, however, it produces a harvest of righteousness and peace for those who have been trained by it. (Heb. 12:7, 10–11)

So how does God want me to react with joy when I'm in a car accident, my husband loses his job, illness or injury strikes my children, tragedy impacts my family, there is serious danger around me in the world, my marriage is teetering on the brink of divorce, or my child is bullied? How am I going to respond as a joyful and peaceful mom when I can't make things better and my children are struggling in some area?

LOOKING FOR THE BEAUTY AND GOOD IN THE MIDST OF TRIALS

Life would be so much easier if there were a formula that we could quickly check to make sure we respond "correctly" in each situation. In my experience, there is no formula, but the first step is always the same—keep my eyes on God. I think God knew that if He gave us too many formulas, we would depend on them rather than learning to depend on and listen to His voice.

If my daughter has an injury at camp, I can pray for her. I can go meet her at the hospital. I can make sure she is getting the care she needs in the emergency room and hold her while she feels so terrible. We can pray together for God to use this situation somehow for His glory and our good. Perhaps we can also thank and praise God together for all the good things we are able to see at the moment. And maybe we can be open together to beautiful things God may have in store in the midst of the trial.

Perhaps there is a person in the ER God wants us to meet or an appointment He has set up for us to share Christ with someone. Or maybe this painful injury will be a way that my daughter and I can bond spiritually as we bring our concerns to Christ. It may be that God uses my example, peace, and joy to bless my daughter and to help instill a strong faith in God in her own life. She may go back to my example in her mind later as she faces more difficult challenges in life.

After I wrote this fictional injury scenario, our ten-year-old daughter actually broke her arm on the first day of summer. First broken bone in our family. We had the chance to practice all the things I have talked about here. I was amazed to see that as I shared with her how she could trust God in this and look for the good God wants to do, she did exactly that.

This trial, and the way we approached it together, brought about more spiritual and emotional growth than I have ever seen in her life before. She had the best attitude about the entire ordeal and usually had a smile on her face once the cast was on. She didn't complain. And ever since her accident, she has had a special place in her heart for others who have broken bones. In fact, for the past three months, she walks right up to other people with casts (especially children) to reach out to them and offer them encouragement. This is the same child who was too shy to talk with strangers before, unless they had a dog with them. We have already seen amazing fruit from her broken arm situation. And there may be much more fruit to come in the future.

> "We can rejoice together over
> the good things God desires
> to bring from the pain."

When my son comes home from school and tells me that someone mistreated him, I can hurt with my son. I can seek to give him godly counsel and involve my husband and the school if necessary. But I can also pray with my son for the classmate who acted in such anger. We can thank God for this trial. We can rejoice together over the good things God desires to bring from the pain. We can pray for God to use this painful situation to possibly bring this child—or my own child—to Christ. We can pray for God to use a bully's hurtful words to teach my son and myself more about forgiveness and how to respond in the power of God's Spirit to those who sin against us. (This doesn't mean my son should trust the bully, of course, unless the bully truly repents.)

This painful thing might open the doors to communication for me to share with my son about living in the Spirit and to brainstorm about the spiritual treasures and lessons God may have for him in this painful place. Perhaps God will use this child's hurtful, hateful words to help my son understand how others feel if he treats them in a similar way, and it may help him to avoid hurting others in the future. Perhaps God will help my son to see that if he responds in the sinful flesh, he is just as wrong as the bully was. If I can keep my eyes on Jesus and look for His hand at work, my children just might get to see some incredible miracles and acts of the Lord.

This could be a pivotal moment in my son's walk of faith and in his life. It could be an opportunity for me to help my son learn to overcome evil with good as Romans 12:17–21 describes. What a perfect opportunity to discuss how God wants us to treat our enemies. Maybe God will show my son that people who hurt and mistreat others are often lost and taken captive by Satan to do his will and that the real enemy is Satan, not the child who lashed out verbally at school.

> For our struggle is not against flesh and blood, but against the rulers, against the authorities, against the powers of this dark world and against the spiritual forces of evil in the heavenly realms. (Eph. 6:12)

Each trial is a test. A chance to practice trusting God, who's promised His love and protection. But we have the opportunity to go way beyond just trusting and waiting on God in faith. God can empower us to develop eyes to see the beautiful treasures to be had in the difficult times. The more we see this, the more we can seriously rejoice when we face difficulties as we immediately begin to look for God's hand at work and the more we can live in His peace in every situation. We can then learn to praise and thank God when things are still dark and we don't know how He will make a way, but we know that He will do it.

Providing an Example in Suffering

There is no more powerful witness for unbelievers (and other believers) than to see a Christian who is suffering, yet praising God and rejoicing even before God's deliverance appears. That is strong faith!

The example of Paul and Silas in prison comes to mind. We never know what adventure God may have in store or what blessings He may drop on us at any moment as we do our part by counting our trials as joy.

> About midnight Paul and Silas were praying and singing hymns to God, and the other prisoners were listening to them. Suddenly there was such a violent earthquake that the foundations of the prison were shaken. At once all the prison doors flew open, and everyone's chains came loose. (Acts 16:25–26)

The Lord used Paul and Silas in mighty ways because of their faith in Him and their willingness to praise Him and depend on Him when they were wrongly imprisoned. All the other prisoners were watching and listening to them. Because of their example and the earthquake God sent, the jailer and his whole family ended up coming into the kingdom of Christ.

Other times, Paul was in prison and God did not deliver him supernaturally like this, but let him remain for long periods of time. And yet, even then, God had His good purposes in mind. God gave Paul that time so he could write over half of the New Testament. He certainly wouldn't have had time to write like this if he had not been confined in a prison cell. When God delivers us, it is for good and beautiful purposes. And when God allows us to remain in a trial for a long period of time, it is also for His good and beautiful purposes. Either way, we can rejoice in Him, in His sovereignty, and in His plans for us.

WHEN FUN PLANS FALL THROUGH —MY STORY

Several years ago, both of our children were really looking forward to going to a fall party at a friend's house one Friday night. Unfortunately, I had to call them with bad news.

I said, "I know y'all were really looking forward to going to this party tonight. Daddy has been working all afternoon to get the new doorknob and lock put in. But he isn't going to be able to get it done in time for us to go to the party, and if I have to drive back home from work to pick you up and take you to the party, we will miss half of it. I know we are all disappointed that we don't get to go to the party tonight.

"You know, sometimes God works things like this out in ways we don't understand at the time. It may be that He has a reason He doesn't want us to go. He may even be protecting us from an accident or something bad. I don't know. I would love for us to trust God's sovereignty tonight and to rejoice in His love for us. Maybe there is something else God desires us to do tonight together?"

Our daughter was pretty young, maybe about five. She calmly told someone later, "It's okay that we can't go to the party tonight. Sometimes it is not God's will for us to do things, but He has something better in store for us. I'm going to color with my crayons."

What an incredible moment to get to teach my children about God's sovereignty and how He uses trials and changes my family's plans to accomplish His purposes, in ways that are beyond our understanding, and that we can trust Him and rejoice in His love for us even when we have to be flexible and even though we feel disappointed at first.

PRAISE CAUSES FEAR TO FLEE —AVA'S STORY

One by one the children got sick. Then I got sick. At two in the morning, I was holding two of them on the couch while sitting up, with trash cans on both sides of us. We were lying on top of beach towels and covered under beach towels to minimize mess and cleanup later.

Vomiting was a bit scary for my toddler, who'd never been sick in that way, and the look in their eyes was so sad. Then I realized I was actually grateful that the four-year-old was now old enough to know he needed to aim for the can or toilet. I felt pathetic. It was pathetic.

And then the Holy Spirit reminded me that we are to count it all joy when we suffer—that we are to praise him through the suffering, and so I started to do just that. "Hallelujah, hallelujah! Glory to God! Worthy is the Lamb!" And the children joined right in! It was uplifting and encouraging, and their sad, scared little eyes turned hopeful and delighted when we sang "This Is the Day the Lord Has Made" in the middle of the night! The Lord blessed us that night and taught us that we should not be discouraged by what is seen, but He drew us to Himself as we looked to what is unseen.

A TRIP TO THE HOSPITAL WITH MY TWO-WEEK-OLD BABY —MY STORY

When our daughter was a tiny infant, she got sick with a fever. I took her to the pediatrician by myself that day while my husband was at work. The fever was 100.3 degrees Fahrenheit, and from the expression on the doctor's face, I knew she was concerned. Apparently, babies under eight weeks of age can't produce a fever much greater than 100 degrees, so it can be difficult to know if they are mildly sick or if it is a really serious infection.

The doctor left the room for a few minutes and then came back and said very apologetically, "I think we need to go ahead and admit your baby into the hospital."

"Okay. I understand," I said and stayed calm. She was shocked that I didn't freak out. (That was a God thing that I didn't freak out, not a me thing.) I walked myself, the baby in the infant carrier, and the diaper bag over to the children's hospital next door and got settled in. I knew that it was a possibility that she could have meningitis or something serious. I also knew that it might just be a virus, probably the one her older brother had the week before.

I stayed with my daughter for three days in the hospital. My husband came to visit when he could. I was still nursing, so I was really thankful that the hospital policy provided meals for the nursing mom. The food was good. We were safe. We had good medical care. I didn't have to leave her side except for during one painful procedure when the doctor wouldn't allow me to stay.

I thought about so many things for which to be thankful. I trusted God and didn't freak out. I tried to think about how I could enjoy the time we shared together in that little room and make sweet memories together. I didn't like seeing her sick, especially at such a young age. But what a blessing that I could be there to take care of her! What a blessing that we had hospital facilities and doctors who could help her if she needed it.

I could have spent those precious hours with my daughter full of anxiety and worry, but that wouldn't have helped her one bit. I'm so glad I decided to look to God with gratitude, joy, and faith even when I didn't know what the outcome would be. I wanted to trust Him whether things went the way I wanted them to go or not.

It turned out that she didn't have any serious infection, and we were able to go home after a few days. But what a gift to know that if my baby got better, if she had some serious illness, or even if the worst were to happen, I could rejoice in the Lord and trust Him no matter what trial I may have to face.

A VISIT TO WASHINGTON, DC, WE WILL NEVER FORGET —MY STORY

In April of 2016, we decided to visit the nation's capitol so that our children could see the museums and experience the history of our country. We were there along with one million other visitors to the city during the weekend of the Cherry Blossom Festival, and the blossoms were at their glorious peak. The crowds were overwhelming everywhere we went, but we enjoyed our visit and were glad our children were old enough to appreciate all of the various sites.

As we were leaving the Capitol building one afternoon, we spoke to the police officer and wished him a good day. Then suddenly, just fifteen seconds or so later, we heard the same police officer behind us yelling, "Get down!" When I looked back, he was diving to the ground behind a wall. I thought maybe he was tackling someone.

Then we heard other police yelling to everyone, "Run! Run!" We ran has hard as we could with other people running near us, not knowing what had happened or how widespread the incident was. One lady called someone on her cell phone as we all ran and said, "A shooting?"

I didn't bring my asthma inhaler that day because the Capitol has gotten very strict about people not bringing in any liquids whatsoever, and I didn't want them to confiscate my rescue inhaler. With the heavy pollen, the panic, and so much sudden running, I began to go into bronchospasm—my lungs felt like they were on fire. I could hardly breathe. After two blocks, I could hardly run anymore.

We saw police streaming into the area from everywhere. Barricades went up on First Street to keep cars out except for police vehicles. Suddenly, the police all had machine guns and were directing everyone away from the Capitol as they ran bravely toward the danger. We made it to the Supreme Court building steps outside and sat down. I tried to catch my breath while a police helicopter swooped directly overhead just above the buildings.

Eventually, we found out that a man brought a pellet gun under his coat, and when the metal detector went off in the security check, he pulled out the gun and aimed it at an officer. The officer quickly shot him, and the man did have to go to the hospital but was later released. We were so grateful to God that the situation was quickly handled and there was no loss of life.

I am extremely glad to know that God is in charge. He has full knowledge and control over the number of each of our days (Ps. 139:16). I trust Him with every detail of our lives and every trial we may face. I'm thankful for His promise to be with us and to never leave us or forsake us—a promise that I could cling to even in the midst of running for our lives and all the chaos that happened that day.

Even in the midst of a terrifying situation where we didn't know what was happening, God was with us at the Capitol. I thought of His promises and sovereignty as we ran. He knew what was happening and what would happen. We can cling to Him and His promises when times are peaceful and even more so when we are surrounded by chaos. Even if something tragic for our family or our country unfolded in those scary moments, I'm so glad that I can trust Him.

These are frightening times, but then they are also perfect times for me to talk with my children about what happened and about God's sovereignty. No matter what we may face, He is ultimately in charge, and He *will* use every situation for our good and His glory because we love Him and are called according to His purpose (Rom. 8:28–29).

If only we can ask God to help us have eyes to see all the reasons to rejoice. When we can rejoice in the midst of great trials, that is a key to being a peaceful mom.

At the bedside of a strong believer in Christ who is dying, there is great joy even in the sorrow. I saw my grandmother's face radiant with joy, and even laughter at times, on her deathbed. It is a beautiful, sacred time—a time when angels are very close and the veil between the earthly and the heavenly becomes extremely thin. It is a time of rejoicing as a Christian runs into the welcoming arms of Jesus. When I am in Christ, I don't have to be afraid of anything, not even death, because Jesus is right there with me.

This is not to say that it is easy or pain-free to have to go through a tragedy. Not at all. None of us want to volunteer for such an assignment. But what peace and joy I can have even in the midst of the most terrible situations because I can rest in God's promises, love, and wisdom.

I think of trials as dark caves sometimes. They can be mines filled with spiritual jewels if I will follow Him and dig deeply where He shows me to dig. He has certain passageways marked off just for me. Yes, the cave is dark, but there I will find precious spiritual gemstones that I can't find anywhere else in life. If only I am receptive and open to His leading, I won't miss these glorious gifts!

My children need to see my faith in this powerful God as we face the scary things that happen in this life. They need to know that our God is so much bigger than any hardship in this world. I can also remind my children and myself that each moment is a precious gift. I want to use the short time I have here on earth wisely. I want to be open to anything God has for me and seek to use even the most difficult situations to allow God to build my faith and my children's faith, that He may use our lives for His greatest glory no matter what the cost. That is the ultimate goal. When I am willing to count trials as joy, and be open to the good the Lord wants to bring from them, I can have supernatural peace as a mom.

GOD IS USING MY UNWANTED
SEPARATION —MICHAEL'S STORY

I went to the Outback for a couple of weeks for work. I strongly suspected that when I got back, my wife would be gone—so it was a hard time. I could see the truth in the thought that a life of faith would be a life of peace, but I couldn't "get" there. I just couldn't. But I knew my iceberg (everything I was trusting in my life—myself, my wife, my marriage, etc.) was melting, and soon I would be drowning.

I took along the book *Absolute Surrender* by Andrew Murray and read it through multiple times. I read Scripture over and over. I took a notepad and wrote down everything that came to my mind, and I realized that I was a massive people pleaser, full of pride and unbelief. I knew I was a Christian, but I was not living in the power of Christ.

It was *not* easy to accept these things about myself, but they were true. Hebrews 3–4 talks about how the same message can be given to two people, and one will benefit from it because he believes it, but another will not benefit because he does not believe it. I could see that rest (the rest God gives us when we trust Him) just sitting there, but I could *not* make myself peaceful.

I came to a point on that last trip where I knew absolutely that my iceberg was going down, and I made a conscious decision to step into the boat of Jesus. I wrote out a prayer of surrender and prayed it. I meant it with my whole heart, but I was a broken, hurting mess. I took a selfie after I had prayed, which was a picture of a broken man with a tearstained face. This may sound weird, but I wanted to remember the sincerity of the commitment. I truly put my idols on the altar that trip and told God that He could have everything for His will. In truth, I was still scared of what He would ask from me, but I was willing to give it. I was probably like the man who cried, "I do believe; help me overcome my unbelief" (Mark 9:24).

God took me at my word. He knew I meant it. And I did mean it. She left. And it hurt. Lots.

I was in the boat with Jesus at the helm, but I was sitting cowering on the floor, shaking with fear and not sure if the boat was going to sink. The enemy was a shark to me, circling around the boat, rubbing against it. I lay in the boat, knowing that I had truly given everything to God but listening to the sound and taunts of the enemy with great fear, still. I could feel the pain of his teeth in my mind. I could hear the storm raging and already feel the pain of the waters of an affair or divorce. But I was committed to trusting God in a conscious decision.

Time passed. I had moments of great peace mixed with moments of great fear. I stopped trying to control things, because I knew I couldn't sail my boat, but I was terrified of where it was going. I listened to the shark and the storm as much as I listened to God. The enemy was out to get me in the biggest way I have ever known before. He did *not* want me to live a life of joy and contentment. I have *never* known so many attacks.

But I saw God's hand through so many situations, and slowly I began to realize that I was not sinking. I remember one situation when I was overwhelmed with fear. I knelt down and cried out to God and said, "God, the Israelites were facing giants and those giants were real! Two of the spies chose to trust Your word, and ten didn't. Maybe those two were still scared, but they chose to trust You! My giants are real, Lord, but I am choosing to trust You even though I am scared!"

Instantly, I felt God's presence and peace and praised Him for that. God is compassionate with our fear.

On a recent trip, I wanted to study boundaries. I had come to a point in my journey where I wanted to be able to create boundaries out of love and strength, not fear. I started reading the Gospels, studying boundaries, and writing down how Jesus dealt with people. I started noticing that all of His dealings with people were done out of a place of great strength and peace, not out of fear. There were times that He let people take advantage of Him and times He did not let them. But it was always done with a purpose and from a place of strength. I knew I was still operating out of fear sometimes, and I knew this was limiting my peace. I started reading a book about spiritual freedom. The Scriptures in that book were Scriptures that God had laid on my heart over the past few months. In so many ways, I see God's hand at work setting me free. I took my notepad again and started writing.

I realized that my biggest fear was abandonment. I was still scared of being alone, and this was limiting me from being truly free. My fear kept me from setting healthy boundaries and stopped me from really enjoying my freedom in Christ. I realized that this fear was the root cause of my people-pleasing behavior. And I realized that even in my little boat, I was scared that Jesus would jump out if I didn't sit in the boat the right way. I surrendered this fear as well. I held up my closed fist to heaven and prayed to God and opened my fist in a picture of letting go of something I was clinging to. I trusted the words of God that He would never abandon me. I trusted, consciously, that if He was willing to give His Son for my salvation, then I would trust Him for everything. And oh, the peace that has come! God is *good*! I took another selfie this trip, only this one was of a man with a peaceful, smiling, radiant face. I wanted to remember this surrender also.

In God's gracious timing, I had let go of all my fear just before the most intense storm of my life hit. Waves are crashing, the wind is howling, sharks are trying to leap into the boat now, but I am sitting in the front of the boat with salt spray on my face, surfing down the waves, fully trusting Jesus at the helm. I am enjoying the ride!

God has brought me so far, and how shall He who spared not His own Son also not freely give us all things! He is working in ways that I would not have anticipated possible—ways that I would never have asked for, but He is working, and His name is going to get so much glory! He is sovereign and allowed me to come to this point of releasing that fear before the next storm hit.

I just love walking with Him. Walking without fear is so good. I wake up in the morning happy, with a smile on my heart. I meet my Savior in prayer and worship each morning. His mercies are renewed every day. I wish I could grab this peace and put it into all of your hearts!

Isaiah 54 has been my constant prayer for my kids through this, particularly verses 13 and 17. I was struck by this passage early on in this journey for many reasons and have claimed protection for my kids as my rightful heritage as a "servant of the Lord." I love that any weapon formed against me "will not prosper" and that God created everything, even the "weapons" that people might use against my kids. This passage describes God's sovereign power over even the situation for my kids and has calmed my heart many times when I think about them.

The storms feel so small in the light of His power. How have I not seen this before? Why do we doubt the infinite power of God when we see His power displayed all around us through creation? My friends are commenting on how peaceful I am. His light is shining, not mine. Rest is good.

I am no longer driven to achieve to earn any favor from Him or from people. I steadily work at the task in front of me for His glory and know that I am secure regardless. I am enjoying my friendships with people so much more. The storms that have hit since I got home have continued to grow. The impact of them is spreading, rippling all around me. The clouds are dark, and the wind is strong.

But I have this calm certainty that the storms in *my heart* are over. They just aren't there anymore. My heart is "different," for want of a better word. I can't explain it properly. I have a peace that is just awesome. And it isn't leaving. A situation rises, and I feel that old fear begin to move, and I consciously look to Christ, and the fear just melts away in the light of the cross. That is where everything centers. It is awesome! It is addictive. I want to walk with God forever. I don't have to know tomorrow because I know my God. These idols are gone, and I don't want them back. I have walked through fear, pain, rejection, and a separation.

Through it all, even when I couldn't see it, God was working to bring good. Not the good of a reunion (yet) or a perfect marriage (yet), but the good of a heart that has a peace not possible without God's strength. That is the treasure worth having. When we wait on the Lord, we truly soar on wings like eagles. It is a testament of what happens when I truly let go of all control and the freedom that results from my being sustained by God's love and presence.

Honestly, if I were relying on my wife in any way, I would have been crushed this last week, and still would be. But God's strength is just so strong. Sisters, God can fill you with a peace that your husbands and other people simply. Can. Not. Give. You. I married as a controlling man, enmeshed in and dependent on an insecure woman. I became a weak and insecure man dependent on a hard woman. Now, I am a strong, secure man, full of the love of Christ and able to give from that heart. God is good!

My friend, Beth, by no means has an easy life. But the other day she wrote me about finding joy in the hard places, and I loved her insights. She wrote:

Look at this small list of the types of things people have done through faith in God and His promises in Hebrews 11:33–38! Not only did they let God bring His kingdom and will into the world through them at any cost—they had Him and His presence in every situation—so that they were more than conquerors no matter what the enemy or the world threw at them. And if the worst happened and they died for Him, He always brought that much more blessing and power and way more people to salvation through it.

What if we knew that through faith we could obtain God's promises, be made strong out of weakness, become mighty in Christ for our spiritual battles, stop the mouth of the enemy lion, and conquer kingdoms? What if we speak Jesus's life and power, breath, hope, and love into darkness? How different our days would be!

I surely would like that kind of strength for myself and my kids. And I daresay you do, too.

A Peaceful Mom's Prayer

Lord,

It does not come naturally to me to see the joy that I could experience with You in trials. But from this moment on, I devote myself to seeking to see trials through Your eyes. Thank You that You are in control of the trials I experience and that You have purposes behind them for my good and for my children's good. Help me to yield in total trust to You in the midst of life's storms. I want to set a godly example for my children so they will learn to look for the spiritual treasures and growth that is available to them in You during the storms of their future. Be glorified in my life. Use me to teach my children well.

Amen.

Living Out Forgiveness, Mercy, and Grace in Our Own Lives

For if you forgive other people when they sin against you,
your heavenly Father will also forgive you. (Matthew 6:14)

We have all seen her. The Ice Queen. That mother with grown children who has been holding on to bitterness for many years, possibly many decades. To cross her, even unintentionally, is the unpardonable sin. She won't allow her husband to speak to their children, even though he has forgiven them and wants to move on. There are no pleasant family dinners, holidays, or friendly conversations anymore. There is only emotional pain and distance. She does all she can to make sure everyone knows they will pay dearly for upsetting her. Maybe for the rest of her life.

When she walks in the room, the atmosphere changes. Coldness settles around her. Laughter and chatting stop. No one smiles. If anyone does, she quickly tries to put a stop to that. People are afraid to speak. Her icy glare communicates to everyone that to enjoy life or relationships around her is to invite personal attack and condemnation. Her bitterness is palpable and oppressive. It has become her core identity after decades of holding on to her grudges. If she has her way, misery is all that is allowed in her presence.

It's a fate that can easily become ours—one in which a lack of forgiveness has hardened into a bitterness that eats away at the core of who we are. The world tries to convince us that when we are wronged, we have a right to be angry and bitter. But let's examine where this path may lead and decide if it is the path we truly want to choose for our families.

Unforgiveness Leads to Bitterness

It is not wrong to be angry when I am sinned against—but in my anger, I am not to sin (Eph. 4:26–27). In Matthew, Jesus talks about a servant who owed his master a large sum of money. The master forgave him and had mercy on him. Then the same servant refused to forgive his fellow slave who owed him a much smaller amount of money.

> Then the master called the servant in. "You wicked servant," he said, "I canceled all that debt of yours because you begged me to. Shouldn't you have had mercy on your fellow servant just as I had on you?" In anger his master handed him over to the jailers to be tortured, until he should pay back all he owed. This is how my heavenly Father will treat each of you unless you forgive your brother or sister from your heart. (Matt. 18:32–35)

When someone offends me, as a peaceful mom, I have a choice. I can feel my pain and then decide to forgive in God's power, or I can ruminate on that sin or mistake. I can dwell on it and meditate on it. I can play it like a movie clip in my mind many times over. When I don't deal with my anger in godly ways, it becomes unrighteous anger, which is a crack in the door that lets Satan have influence and power in my life. The longer I allow this to continue, the greater the enemy's hold over me.

When unforgiveness becomes a chronic situation, it ferments into bitterness, which is much more difficult to tear out of our hearts than simple unforgiveness. I like www.gotquestions.org's definition of *bitterness*:

> Bitterness is resentful cynicism that results in an intense antagonism or hostility towards others. . . . As an adjective, the word *bitter* means "sharp like an arrow or pungent to the taste, disagreeable; venomous." . . . In its figurative sense *bitterness* refers to a mental or emotional state that corrodes or "eats away at." Bitterness . . . acts on the mind in the way poison acts on the body.[7]

A Bitter Mom's Heart

If I choose to be bitter, I choose to keep track of all the wrongs my children have committed against me. I nurture my hurt and pain and keep rehashing each offense in my heart. I savor resentment against my children. I view my unforgiveness as my special right against them as I view them as evil (or at least as "wrong") and myself as an innocent victim. If I do something for them, I make sure they know that I am doing it as a martyr, as we talked about in chapter 9, or that I resent anything good I may do for them. I let them know they don't deserve my love, gifts, or forgiveness.

I won't accept any of my children's apologies to me. Nothing they can do is good enough to satisfy my anger and to entice me to forgive them. I won't receive their love. I also withhold my love as punishment against them for hurting me. I am the gatekeeper of my relationship with my children, and in my bitterness, I increasingly refuse to allow any love through in either direction. I don't want love anymore. I want to be the judge. I want to condemn and accuse them.

My bitterness will lead me to feel compelled to tell everyone around me about how ungrateful my children are and how much they have hurt me. I want everyone to have a negative view of my children and a positive view of me. I will feel justified in gossiping about them and even slandering them, because they hurt me first, after all. I want other people to share my bitterness toward my children. I may even try to get my grandchildren to side with me against their parents.

Bitterness, left unchecked, eventually becomes deadly.

My bitterness will lead me to increasingly deadly attitudes. I will move from resentment to hatred to malice. Malice is where I want to hurt my children because they have hurt me. First, I may seek to hurt them emotionally with my attitudes, words, and actions, which is emotional abuse. I become the ice queen mom that no one wants to be around.

But eventually, I may even want to physically hurt others. Unchecked malice leads to violence and physical abuse. As I continue to allow my bitterness to have its way in my heart, it ultimately leads to thoughts of murder, and then it can lead to actual murder. This is exactly why there are stories on the news every day in which a supposed loved one is killed by a family member. Bitterness, when given free reign, eventually becomes deadly.

Here are some causes of bitterness:

Pride
Unmet expectations
Idolatry of someone's
    approval
Idolatry of self, others, or
    desires
A desire to control others
Assuming evil motives

Being sinned against
Different perspectives
Different personal convictions
Ignoring sin in others or self
Selfishness
Cherishing my anger
Jealousy
Unbelief/lack of faith in God

Defining Terms

Before we go any further, let's define a few things so we are all on the same page.

Forgiveness means I don't count someone's offense against that person anymore. I recognize that what the person did to me was wrong. I don't pretend it was okay. Then, I purposely decide not to hold this thing in my heart against my offender. I don't hold a grudge. I don't try to get revenge. I am released from sinful thoughts on my end. And I am not a prisoner of resentment. I trust God to bring about justice for the situation in His timing. Forgiveness is not the same thing as trust or reconciliation. I can forgive someone who has not repented. But I can't trust someone who is continuing in unrepentant sin against me. Trust is conditional. Forgiveness is unconditional.

Mercy means I don't receive something bad that I deserve. God gave me mercy by laying my punishment for my sin on Jesus. He received all the condemnation and punishment I deserved. If I am extending mercy to my child, it means I don't try to take vengeance on him. It means I don't try to pay back evil for evil. I don't give him something bad that he may deserve. I would still need to appropriately discipline him. But I would continue to love him and not withdraw my love from him.

Grace means I receive something good that I don't deserve. God gives me salvation, a new life in Christ, intimacy with Him spiritually, and an inheritance with Christ in heaven. I don't deserve any of that. I deserve hell for my sin. I might give grace to my child by loving her unconditionally, always being open to relationship with her, doing things I know will ultimately be best for her.

Why Is Bitterness Wrong?

We've established why we don't want to harbor unforgiveness (who wants to be a lonely ice queen?). The world describes bitterness as a "right" and "privilege." So could it really be that bad?

Here are just a handful of Scriptures about God's position on bitterness:

- God will not forgive me if I don't forgive others' sins against me (Matt. 6:14–15).
- It is fruit of the sinful flesh and leads to division, factions, dissensions, and so forth (Gal. 5:18–21).
- It gives Satan access to my life (Eph. 4:26–27).
- It grieves the Spirit of God (Eph. 4:30–31).
- It is a gateway to sin that leads to many other sins and contaminates other people as well (Heb. 12:14–15).

When I hold on to anger and nurse a grudge—I create a cozy, welcoming place for Satan, or his demons, to enter into my life and relationships. I let him set up camp in my heart and attack my family and myself through my thoughts, attitudes, words, and actions. I cooperate with the enemy and resist God's work in my heart. What a dangerous place to be!

Fruit of Bitterness in My Own Life

Bitterness leads to very specific results in my life that are easy to recognize (though some of these things can have other causes as well):

- Tension and anxiety about seeing that person
- Depression
- Insomnia
- Other stress-related health problems
- Disrespect
- Lack of self-control
- A desire to avoid the person
- Vengeance
- Lack of compassion

- Lack of desire to pray for the person
- Withholding affection
- Unfriendliness
- Fear of conflict or confrontation
- A strong desire for conflict/confrontation
- Lack of desire for God
- Annoyance
- A judgmental spirit toward the other person
- Complaining
- Arguing
- Discontentment
- Idolatry of self and of my bitterness
- Vilification of the other person
- An eventual seared conscience
- A feeling that God's Word and my quiet time have turned dry
- The loss of the fruit of God's Spirit in my life (until I repent)
- My love growing cold
- Total loss of influence and witness for Christ
- Violence against the other person or myself

How Does My Bitterness Against Others Affect My Children?

If I hold on to resentment toward my husband, my children, or anyone else in my life, not only do I poison my own heart with sin, but I also contaminate my children's hearts as well. I model for them that bitterness is justifiable. I may even draw them into my own personal relationships to try to get them to side with me against whomever I resent.

Here are some ways my bitterness against others hurts my children:

- I try to destroy their love for that person.
- I teach them dysfunctional ways of relating to others.
- I model unhealthy conflict resolution.
- I encourage them to hate another family member.

- I teach them that they are "wrong" if they love me and the other family member.
- I single-handedly make our home or extended family life a war zone where my children do not feel safe.
- I teach them not to obey God but to trust self instead, which is actually trusting Satan.
- I encourage them to take revenge rather than believing God will handle vengeance because it belongs to Him.
- I model hatred and contempt that is not compatible with the lordship of Christ—this can cause great confusion if I am trying to teach them to live as Christians and to obey God.

How Does My Bitterness Toward My Children Destroy Our Relationship?

There are few relationships as powerful as the relationship between a mother and her children. If I choose to hold bitterness against my children for decades, the damage I can create is incalculable.

- I model for them that love is conditional.
- They may no longer be able to experience love from me. It is almost impossible for my children to receive love from me if I resent, accuse, and judge them.
- I may repel them and sabotage any emotional or spiritual intimacy we could share.
- They may dread being around me.
- This is a path that eventually leads to estrangement and no communication.

If I Am Bitter at My Children, They Are More Likely to Have Trouble Having Healthy Relationships

I am not responsible for my children's choices and their sin. However, I can greatly impact their understanding of how to relate to other people in healthy ways. I can set a destructive example that creates quite a stumbling block for them, or I can set a godly example that creates a holy example for them to model. If I hold great bitterness against my children, these things could happen:

- They may learn to use the same dysfunctional coping techniques they use with me in other relationships.
- They may not be able to receive love very well from anyone else.
- They may think that having an emotionally abusive relationship is normal.
- They may learn to try to be people pleasers.
- They may decide to become very selfish and not even try to do things to bless others because it seems impossible to have a healthy relationship.
- They may have trouble trusting a future spouse or understanding how to have a healthy marriage.
- They may model my approach when they have their own children and hurt their own relationships with their future children as well, continuing my destructive legacy.

How Do I Overcome Bitterness?

The earlier I tear bitterness out of my thoughts, the easier it is. If I can catch it when it is still a temptation to unrighteous anger or unforgiveness, that is ideal. Then I can just quickly shoot down the sinful thought before it begins to fester in my heart. This is possible when I am allowing God's Spirit to have control in my heart and I have fellowship with Him. The longer bitterness sits in my heart, the more that little root grows into a big, ugly, evil tree that consumes my soul and infects those around me.

See to it . . . that no bitter root grows up to cause trouble and defile many. (Heb. 12:15)

I picture lying still before God on the operating table as He opens up my heart and examines every dark crevice with the blazing Light of His Word and truth. He is looking for the cancer and gangrene that bitterness and sinful thoughts bring. Even though it is painful at the moment, this is the way to healing. I used to try to get rid of my bitter thoughts, but I didn't understand that I needed to replace them with godly thoughts. No wonder I struggled so much for so long! As with any sinful thought pattern, I must get rid of the poison and then receive God's truth and rebuild on that. I need God to renew my mind by the power of His truth and His Word. I must allow Him to show me every offensive way in me. It all has to go ASAP.

This is a (fictional) example of how I might approach the Lord if I have been wronged by my children:

First, I would tell God what's happening and how I feel about it. *I felt so angry at my children today. They were fighting and being so disrespectful to me and to each other. I asked them to stop, but the whining, fussing, and bickering went on and on. Eventually, I completely lost my temper and yelled at them without any self-control.*

Second, as I talk to God, I might start to see why I'm angry and I might list those reasons—all that I can think of. *God, I feel angry because:*

I want my children to be kind and respectful to each other.
I want them to respect me.
I want them to obey like they are supposed to.
I want them to reflect well on me.
I am embarrassed when we are in public and they go off on each other or treat me with disrespect.
I am afraid they will never change and will always continue with this awful pattern.
I want them to be perfect and never mess up.

Third, I do not hesitate to point out the areas that are clearly God's will. *And, God, I want Your good things for my kids:*

> *You want my children to obey me and to treat each other well.*
> *You want my children to respect each other and people in positions of authority in their lives, including me.*
> *You want my children to grow in godliness and spiritual maturity.*
> *You want them to have a healthy relationship.*

Fourth, I move into confession. I lay bare my sin, revealing where I fell short of being the peaceful mom God intended. *But, Lord, I do see that some of my motives here were wrong:*

> *I had fear about what other people were thinking in the store.*
> *I had pride going on because I am embarrassed for anyone to see that my children aren't perfect in public.*
> *I had unrealistic expectations of my children.*
> *I was not responding in the Spirit but reacting in the flesh.*

I humbly repent to You, and I will repent to my children after this prayer time. I turn away from anything You call sin, and I run to You in my mind. I repent of any inappropriate, toxic anger in my heart. Cleanse me of my sin by Your blood. I receive Your forgiveness, mercy, and grace for myself. Pour all of that goodness through me and let me extend it to my children. Get rid of every evil thought in me.

Fifth, I move forward in Christ's strength. *I refuse to believe Satan's lies that I should resent my children and not forgive them. Yes, they wronged each other, You, and me. But I choose Your wisdom and Your ways. I need to be forgiven myself, even today. I am not better than my kids. Without Jesus, there is no good in any of us.*

Help me have Your power to obey You, even though it would feel

good for a while to cling to unforgiveness, I know where that would lead,
and it is so not worth it! I surrender every bit of my unrighteous anger
and unforgiveness to You. I forgive my children for their behavior today
because You forgive me for my sin. I praise and thank You for all that You
are about to do in my life and in my children's lives. Amen!

I Can Only Extend as Much Grace and Forgiveness as I Have Received

I used to believe that I really didn't "sin that much" and didn't owe
God much of a debt. So I thought to myself, "I will never be able to love
Jesus as much as those people who sinned greatly against Him." Oh,
how big my pride was before my fall.

Then, for the first time, in December 2008, God peeled away the
layers of my false sense of goodness. I came face-to-face with the fact
that I was a wretched sinner—even though I had received Christ as a
five-year-old child. I began to see exactly how incalculable my debt was
to God and exactly how much Jesus had paid on my behalf on the cross.

I had more than a "beam" in my own eye. It seemed to me that it was
a forest!

- I had my husband, children, self, and being in control as idols.
- I did not love God wholeheartedly.
- My heart was full of pride.
- I seriously thought I had a corner on knowing God's will that
  other people just couldn't have.
- I held on to grudges against everyone. I felt like I could not forgive
  people even when I wanted to.
- I couldn't extend grace to my children.
- I thought I trusted God, but I really didn't.
- I tried to override my family's free will.
- I lived like God was tiny and wimpy.
- I unknowingly tried to take on God's sovereignty for myself.

- I unknowingly believed a lot of lies about God, others, and myself.
- Fear and anxiety fueled my choices as a mom.
- I was prickly and difficult to live with.
- I was easily offended and upset.
- I had a lot of bitterness and resentment.
- I gossiped often.
- I was negative and had a critical spirit.
- I was contentious.
- The way I responded to my children escalated everyone's tension.
- I looked down on everyone else as being so much less spiritually mature than I was.
- I set a disrespectful example for my children in the way I related to my husband and to other adults.
- I was so impatient with my children and got exasperated easily.
- I lost my temper with my children when we were running late, which was often.
- I found ways to justify anything sinful in my heart.

I thought back to all the passages in the Old Testament about idolatry that I had ignored because I didn't think I had that issue. Idolatry is a serious thing in God's eyes. To Him, me committing idolatry against Him is similar to me committing adultery in marriage. And I had put these other things and people above Christ in my heart every waking moment for decades! Yikes! That was a really big deal. Actually, all of these sins were a big deal.

It hit me just how much Jesus really paid for my sin on the cross. I owed Him more than I could ever understand. What incredible love Jesus has for me! It was not until I saw the depths of my own sin and depravity and truly experienced God's amazing grace for myself that I was able to begin to extend a bit of this kind of extravagant mercy, grace, and forgiveness toward others. This is how humility changes me and enables me to begin to love with God's love.

When I see another person's sin against me, I can recognize that it hurts me and it is wrong. But then I can look to God's example in how He dealt with my sin. I can acknowledge that this person's sin against me is wrong, like my sins against others and against the Lord. I can see what a great debt I owed God that I could never repay. I can see the price God paid to cover my sin and make me right with Him. What the other person did against me, even if it was bad, is a very small thing compared to my mountain of sin against the Lord. So I can ask God to give me His eyes to see those who sin against me—that I might see that they are trapped in Satan's snare and need to be set free, like I needed to be set free.

I then humbly acknowledge that only Jesus is good. I have no goodness in myself. Apart from God, I am capable of any sin. So I can then extend the grace I have received so lavishly from God to those who sin against me. I can also see that God calls me to forgive for my own benefit and that unforgiveness and bitterness are a trap and a snare of the enemy of my soul.

Learning to Forgive Even That

I vividly remember seeing the coverage on the news about the shooting at Sandy Hook Elementary School in Connecticut on December 14, 2012. Our daughter was in kindergarten at the time, and I could just so easily picture a disturbed young man walking into her classroom and shooting her and her friends for no reason.

I thought, "I know that God calls on me to forgive even if someone were to kill my child. Wow. How I hope that I will never be tested to that degree! What could be worse than someone killing my child and having to forgive that person? Unless, maybe, they tortured my child first." Then God immediately spoke to me quietly in my thoughts: "That is exactly what I have forgiven you for, April."

"*What?* What was that, Lord?"

"Your sin put My Son on the cross. My Son died at your hands. And

He didn't just die—He was tortured and died a slow, cruel, agonizing death. Not only that, He carried all your sin on His sinless shoulders and paid for every one of them. And I completely forgave you."

That left me speechless.

The list of my offenses weighed heavily on my shoulders. God had forgiven me my extensive list, and yet I struggled to forgive infinitely smaller offenses. What if one day, God asks me to forgive something as awful as the shooting at Sandy Hook Elementary School? I pray that none of us might have to face such a situation. But I know that my Lord—the Author of forgiveness—can empower me to forgive anything. I trust that He will enable me to do so if that day comes.

When I think about forgiveness, there are three things that help me.

The first is looking at it from Jesus's perspective on the cross: "Father, forgive them, for they do not know what they are doing" (Luke 23:34). It helps me to keep in mind that when people sin egregiously against us, they usually don't know what they are doing. They are generally blinded by sin and Satan, held captive to do his will. If they could see sin as God sees it, and if they had His Spirit's power, they wouldn't do it!

The second is examining Joseph's incredible example of forgiveness in the Old Testament—when he forgave his brothers who sold him into slavery. I love that when he revealed himself to his brothers, over fourteen years after they betrayed him, he said, "You intended to harm me, but God intended it for good to accomplish what is now being done, the saving of many lives" (Gen. 50:20). What comfort there is in knowing that our powerful, sovereign Lord can take even the most evil intentions of people and use all of it ultimately for our good, for His glory, and for His kingdom's work!

> Bless those who persecute you; bless and do not curse. . . . Do not repay anyone evil for evil. Be careful to do what is right in the eyes of everyone. If it is possible, as far as it depends

on you, live at peace with everyone. Do not take revenge, my dear friends, but leave room for God's wrath, for it is written: "It is mine to avenge; I will repay," says the Lord. On the contrary: "If your enemy is hungry, feed him; if he is thirsty, give him something to drink. In doing this, you will heap burning coals on his head." Do not be overcome by evil, but overcome evil with good. (Rom. 12:14, 17–21)

Finally, there will be justice. Those who sin against me will turn to Christ Jesus and He will pay for their sins against me with His innocent, perfect, holy blood, or they will pay for their sins themselves in hell forever, according to the Bible—which is the only source of absolute truth. I don't want *anyone* to end up in hell! Not even my enemies. How I pray they will each come to know Christ!

> There will be justice, ultimately, for the wrongs we have suffered.

I cannot help but respond with humility, true repentance, and gratitude toward Him when I see what the Lord has done for me! And then, when God asks me to forgive, out of gratefulness, I find it easier to respond in the same manner toward those who sin against me (Matt. 18:21–35). When God empowers me to be able to respond with forgiveness, mercy, and grace, I get to experience so much peace as a mom. There is no peace in bitterness, grudges, malice, and hatred. There is peace in love, mercy, grace, and forgiveness.

Grace as a Witness

What a powerful witness for Christ when believers extend mercy, grace, and forgiveness, rather than hatred and bitterness. Think about the example of the church in Charleston, South Carolina, in June 2015, when Dylann Roof shot and killed nine of their members during a

Wednesday night Bible study. These believers forgave the man who murdered their loved ones.

What he did was awful—the very epitome of evil! It was totally inexcusable and completely unjustified. But what they did was supernatural. Because of their beautiful example, the gospel was proclaimed and exalted around the world on secular news stations! The world was confused, shocked, and intrigued by these believers' godly response.

Or think about the people from the Preemptive Love Coalition in Iraq in 2016, led by Matt Willingham. Willingham determined, against the will of Iraqi leaders, to give food, water, clothing, and aid to hundreds of former ISIS soldiers who were being detained by Iraqi officials. "We believe only light can drive out darkness. . . . Love is the only real answer to hate. So we went anyway—and gave food, water and clothing to hundreds of high-risk detainees in the compounds outside Fallujah," Willingham wrote on his blog.[8]

Love drives out hate in our churches, our communities, and our nations. But that love has to start somewhere. Most likely, it needs to start right here in my heart and in my family. Am I ready to allow God to use me to shine for Him, too, in my little corner of the world? If I am willing to obey Him and not hold on to bitterness, what miracles might God have in store in my life, my family, His kingdom, and for bringing the lost to Himself? And what peace my children and I will get to experience!

FORGIVENESS IS NOW A "FAMILY AFFAIR" —JACKIE'S STORY

Ever since the Lord has opened my eyes to all my own sin, He has been working in my relationship with my son and in me as well—specifically, He's been teaching me how to not only extend forgiveness, mercy, and grace to my son, but also how to ask for forgiveness from him when I am wrong and I mess up.

The Lord is also using my husband and me to show my son how to extend mercy and grace by the way we apologize to each other and our whole family when things get out of hand. Anytime I am having a moment, or am hormonal, tired, stressed, and not walking in the Spirit, I am bound to start hurting my family by being negative, using a bossy or mean tone of voice, and most likely losing my cool in some way.

Over the past several months, any time I have been found in this condition and I have hurt my son or my husband by my own sinful behavior, the Lord has not let me get away with it. His Spirit in me has been faithfully convicting me every time I am wrong, and until I apologize to my family, I have a bad time! So for a while now, I have been able to experience this firsthand; whenever I am wrong, I have been led to immediately make it right by apologizing to my husband and son and asking their forgiveness. My son then gets to witness my husband forgiving me and showing me love even when I don't deserve it. And my son learns to extend grace and mercy even when I don't deserve it. It even seems like it is easier for my son to forgive me unconditionally than for anyone else I know! He is so quick to forgive, and he never holds grudges. His heart is soft and full of love!

The same is true for my son when he is caught in any sin and is sent to his room to think about it. He usually has a meltdown first about it, and lately the Lord has truly been working in my heart to help me remain calm when my son is out-of-control at home, and just calmly let him know that when he is able to calm down then we can talk about it.

My son is having fewer and fewer tantrums and is able to control himself and calm down a lot faster now, too. And when he calms down, he will come to me and speak kindly and apologize. I no longer get mad or freak out on him. I simply say that I love him and forgive him, that I'll always love him, and that I am proud of him for doing the right thing. And we hug, and proceed from there.

I see such a change in the way my family interacts now. When my husband is wrong, he will usually go for a drive, come home, and apologize to my son for not acting right. Then he apologizes to me for how he acted if it was wrong toward me. And then we have a family hug, and my son loves nothing more than to see my husband and me on the same ground of love. We all make it a point to not only give grace to each other, but to seek it from each other when we know we are wrong! The Lord is honored by this, and when the Lord is honored, true miracles start happening!

HOW I CHOSE FORGIVENESS AND DEFUSED A POTENTIALLY EXPLOSIVE MOMENT —HEATHER'S STORY

By Saturday most weeks, I get pretty weary. All week long I wake up at four in the morning to get my husband off to work, and then I get some time with the Lord before getting my son off to school. But by Saturdays, I am pretty spent. Well, this past Saturday, for example, we were all home and I was not feeling up to par. I got overly upset when my husband said he was going to take a nap. I tried to take one, too, but—no success.

My husband fell asleep on the couch for hours, and my seven-year-old son was his hyper self. My son told me he was hungry about twenty times, and I snapped. Grouchy, tired, and irritated, I snapped and told him to *stop* telling me he is hungry every three minutes, and to just grab a snack. This woke my husband up. I spiraled downhill from there, and ended up alone, in my room, mumbling about how much my family aggravates me. Lying on my bed, I heard the Spirit in my heart say, "That was *not* Christ—that was *you*!" And I could not shake it off. I couldn't stay in my room. I knew I was wrong.

I came out, denied myself, denied the bitterness that was trying to overtake my heart, and called my son to me. I knelt down and said, "I'm sorry. What I did was wrong. I shouldn't have snapped at you like that. There's no excuse. Will you forgive me?"

He said, "I forgive you," gave me a big hug, and skipped away, his usual happy self.

I apologized to my husband and told him I was obviously tired and it was not my best day. I asked him to forgive me in front of my son, of course, and he said he forgave me. He didn't get mad. He didn't shut down emotionally. He showed compassion and told me that it's best we all just relax and go to bed early. We all went to bed without any anger or bitterness or unforgiveness in our hearts. We are not perfect. But we are learning by the grace of God, and Christ is being formed in us as we go.

GOD CALLS ME TO FORGIVE

It is a good thing to hate what is wrong. God hates sin wholeheartedly, after all. One of His eternal character traits is that He is just. He must ensure that right wins against any evil. The problem for me, in my humanness, is that not only does God want me to hate sin like He does, but He also commands me to completely forgive those who sin against me. Even if they don't apologize or repent. That is hard. Really hard. Maybe I would even say—humanly impossible.

God knows that forgiveness and grace are critical for any relationship with an imperfect person. Without it, genuine intimacy with any human is impossible. Jesus's life in us makes us right with God. Once we have received Jesus's forgiveness, mercy, and grace, then His Spirit empowers us to extend the same to others. He invites us to participate in His kind of unconditional love as we learn to love the unlovable, even when they are our own children. Trust may have to be rebuilt because trust is conditional. But we don't have to be stuck in the dungeon of unforgiveness or bitterness. Jesus gives us the ability to be truly peaceful moms.

A Peaceful Mom's Prayer

Lord,

I choose to forgive my children, my husband, and anyone else who has sinned against me. I know I can't do this on my own. I ask You to work this miracle in me by Your power. I trust You, and I lay my bitterness at Your feet. I want to get rid of every bit of it. Cleanse me. Help me to remember that I am dead to my sinful self and this world and alive to God through Jesus. Help me live by the new nature You have provided for me and make no room for bitterness in my heart. Empower me to choose to live a life of love, mercy, grace, and forgiveness for Your glory!

Amen.

Conclusion

The path to becoming a peaceful mom is a lifelong journey of discipleship in Christ that is painful at times. I long to yield myself totally to God, His wisdom, His lordship, and His ways. What priceless spiritual rewards await me in this life and the next as I follow Him. Then I get to live in His power rather than the power of self. It is the adventure of a lifetime and my greatest joy to experience the Prince of Peace in my life in multifaceted ways.

Through Jesus, I receive peace in so many areas of my life:

- Between God and myself so that I don't have to fear condemnation and hell
- In my relationship with God so that I can have true intimacy with Him
- In my heart in the midst of trying circumstances, suffering, and the unknown
- In my thoughts as I take them captive for Christ
- In my soul as I lay down my fears and my dreams and trust God to accomplish His purposes and His good plans for my family and me
- In all my human relationships, including with my children, as far as it depends on me

I have never regretted my decision to follow Christ wholeheartedly and to allow Him to radically transform my heart, mind, and life. This is truly the only way I know to be a peaceful mom. I pray that you will continue to join me on this incredible journey. How exciting to see all that God has in store for each of us who take this narrow way. May we walk this ancient path together and show our children the way to become peaceful in Jesus as well.

Appendix A

How to Have a Saving Relationship with Jesus Christ

If you don't have a relationship with Jesus or you are not sure if you do, I invite you to find out what He offers to you and how you can know Him as your Savior and Lord today. Then you can have the peace of knowing you are right with God and will not face condemnation or hell when this life is over, and you can begin to experience the blessings of knowing and loving God in everyday life.

Who Is God?

According to the Bible—our primary source for absolute truth about who God is and who we are—there is one God who has always existed outside time and space. He is completely perfect, loving, kind, good, powerful, holy, majestic, wise, and just. He can't do anything wrong or be tempted to do anything that is evil. He created all that exists from nothing and made our world, plants, animals, and people just as Genesis 1 describes. He began with two people, Adam and Eve, the first husband and wife. But God did not want mindless robots who had to obey Him and didn't have a choice. So He gave people free will so that their love for Him and for others would be meaningful.

Sadly, Adam and Eve chose to rebel against God in the garden of Eden when they ate from the tree from which God had commanded them not to eat. The world that had been so good became corrupted by sin. From that point on, we have had sickness, natural disasters, war, death, and suffering because sin entered the world. We have all been contaminated by sin through Adam and Eve. God promised them a Savior even then—someone who would defeat Satan, sin, and death. He already had a plan—before He ever created the world and before people rebelled against Him—for how He was going to reclaim His fallen, beloved people for Himself.

WHAT IS SIN?

Sin means "missing the mark" of the holy standard of God. The Hebrew word for "sin," *hata*, was an archery term that means that the arrow missed the target. If the arrow missed the target by half an inch, that is a sin. If it missed it by a hundred yards, that is also a sin.

There are many sins. Here are a few:

Greed	Rage
Selfishness	Slander
Lust	Self-righteousness
Idolatry (putting something before God in our hearts)	Boasting
	Apathy
Stealing	Hatred
Gluttony	Bitterness
Pride	Grudges
Unbelief	Disobeying God's Word
Unforgiveness	Gossip
Envy	Addiction of any kind
Taking God's name in vain	Abuse
Adultery/sexual immorality	False religion
Lying	Forsaking God

All these things separate me far from the one and only holy God of the universe and tragically keep me from being able to have a relationship with Him (Isa. 59:2). God is perfectly holy and undefiled. One act of rebellion against Him, even just in my thoughts, is enough for me to "miss the mark." "For all have sinned and fall short of the glory of God" (Rom. 3:23).

WHAT DOES GOD SAY ABOUT OUR SIN? HOW DOES HE DEAL WITH IT?

God is completely pure, sinless, and perfect, and He is perfectly just. He must demand proper payment for wrongs that have been done. He will not allow injustice. I am thankful that God doesn't ignore sin and that He brings about justice. That is right and good, but this is a huge problem for me as a sinner. No one is able to be good enough to earn his or her way to be with God in heaven. "All of us have become like one who is unclean, and all our righteous acts are like filthy rags" (Isa. 64:6). Our best behavior on our own is like filthy, bloody menstrual rags in God's sight. The Bible says this:

- Jesus replied, "Very truly I tell you, no one can see the kingdom of God unless they are born again" (John 3:3).
- Jesus answered, "I am the way and the truth and the life. No one comes to the Father except through me" (John 14:6).
- All have sinned and fall short of the glory of God (Rom. 3:23).
- For the wages of sin is death, but the gift of God is eternal life in Christ Jesus our Lord (Rom. 6:23).
- If you declare with your mouth, "Jesus is Lord," and believe in your heart that God raised him from the dead, you will be saved. For it is with your heart that you believe and are justified, and it is with your mouth that you profess your faith and are saved. As Scripture says, "Anyone who believes in him will never be put to shame" (Rom. 10:9–11).

- Now, brothers and sisters, I want to remind you of the gospel I preached to you, which you received and on which you have taken your stand. By this gospel you are saved, if you hold firmly to the word I preached to you. . . . For what I received I passed on to you as of first importance: that Christ died for our sins according to the Scriptures, that he was buried, that he was raised on the third day according to the Scriptures (1 Cor. 15:1–4).
- And he died for all, that those who live should no longer live for themselves but for him who died for them and was raised again (2 Cor. 5:15).
- For it is by grace you have been saved, through faith—and this not from yourselves, it is the gift of God—not by works, so that no one can boast (Eph. 2:8–9).
- Here I am! I stand at the door and knock. If anyone hears my voice and opens the door, I will come in and eat with that person, and they with me (Rev. 3:20).

THE HOLY HERO

When I was unable to do anything about my sinful, wretched condition and was still dead spiritually in my sins, Jesus was willing to set aside His glory as God, take on a human body, live a perfect life as a man, and then take the unfathomable weight of the sin of the entire world onto His pure, undefiled, holy soul on the cross. He fully paid the penalty that I had earned. He bore the colossal weight of every sin ever committed and overcame death to rescue each of us—if I will but accept His gift, put my trust and faith in Him, love Him with my whole heart, and yield my life to His lordship. I can't earn this relationship or this love. He is willing to take my sin and the death I deserved and give me His life, His right relationship with God, His holiness, His power, His heaven . . . Wow! That is truly the most amazing love story ever told.

- He lived the perfect life I could not live.
- He died the awful death I deserved.
- He took all my sin onto Himself and paid for it in full. He is the only one who was worthy and able to do this.
- He offers to exchange all of His goodness and righteousness for all of my sinfulness.
- He gets what I deserve, and I get what He deserves. That is not fair at all. That is *grace*!
- He gave all for me.
- Now I give all of myself to Him from this moment onward in gratitude, to live for Him and to seek His will and His glory.
- I don't earn salvation by anything I do. I just respond to His gift with thanksgiving and desire to please Him.

Jesus's Longing for Us

He longs for each of us to love Him with all that we are—to worship Him as the Lord of our lives, the one who is in charge. He longs for us to follow Him, delight in Him, praise Him, thank Him, worship Him, and reverence Him every day. He wants us to trust Him and put all our faith in Him alone rather than in the things and people of this world, who will only disappoint us.

He desires to love us, lead us, cherish us, make us more and more like Him, and be one Spirit with us. He wants to connect with us 24/7, for us to know Him deeply and intimately. He wants to prepare us to be His radiant, sinless, spotless bride in heaven (Eph. 5:27)—where a great wedding feast awaits all who love and trust in Him!

But He will not force us to love Him. He is a gentleman, and He gave us free will so we can choose to love or reject Him and His gift of life with Him as His bride forever. We will not physically unite with Him in a one-flesh relationship as in an earthly marriage, but in a one-spirit relationship together with all who love Jesus.

LOSING THE SHACKLES OF SIN

I pray that you might be sensitive to God's Holy Spirit speaking to your heart today. There is no sin that Jesus's blood cannot cleanse from our souls. None of us are beyond His reach. I pray that you might repent (turn one hundred eighty degrees away from sin and toward Jesus) and live for Him by faith in all that He has done for you from this day on!

This is how you can throw off the weight of sin that entangles you! I pray that you will say "Yes!" to His invitation to be your Savior and Lord—the one who deeply knows you yet loves you anyway, the one from whom you have no secrets and no room to brag. I pray that you will say "Yes!" to the one who gave up His life and suffered and died in your place—paying for your sins—so you could live a spiritually abundant life now and live with Him happily ever after in heaven forever! I pray you will discover how good the Lord Jesus is and find His narrow path that leads to life.

FOLLOW UP

If you are interested in giving your heart and life to Jesus, you are welcome to leave a comment on my blog—or you can read more in your Bible or speak to a strong Bible-believing Christian or Bible-believing pastor who can tell you more. You can have a loving relationship with the King of Kings and Lord of Lords that will give you life forever in heaven with Him in the future, and a life of spiritual abundance, adventure, forgiveness, peace, joy, and freedom here on earth.

This first step, when God gives me new spiritual life, is called "salvation" or being "born again."

1. I turn totally away from anything God calls sin.
2. I put my faith in what Jesus has done for me—His death, burial, and resurrection.
3. I receive Him as my Savior and Lord.

I invite Him to be in charge, and I yield my life and all that I have to Him in gratitude for all He has done for me on the cross.

At that moment, Jesus puts all His goodness in my account, and my debt to God is paid completely. I live for Him from this point on. As I continue to grow and mature in Him, He provides me with the power of His Spirit. I seek to know Him more deeply, to allow Him to radically change me to be more and more like Him, to walk in obedience to Him (by His power working in me), and to bring Him the greatest glory in all that I do.

When I am willing to trash anything that is sinful in my life and receive all that God has for me, I am able to be truly beautiful spiritually in the eyes of God! I can have the gentle, peaceful spirit that does not give way to fear—the spirit that is so gorgeous and lights me up with the joy of Jesus! That is when I soar on wings like an eagle and live life to its absolute fullest!

Appendix B

Some "Proofs" That I Belong to Christ and That His Spirit Is Working in My Heart

If I am in Christ, His Spirit works in me to change me and to conform me into His image. I would expect to see an increase in my life of things such as these:

- I deeply want God to change me, cleanse me, and make me more like Jesus.
- I begin to hate my sin.
- I am willing to learn to trust Him with everything, and I want to give up my sense of control—which is just an illusion, anyway.
- I am willing to submit to Him—meaning He is in charge now, not me. I voluntarily enthrone Him as Lord of my life. He is the Master.
- I am willing to seek His will above my own.
- I realize His wisdom is much greater than mine.
- I see Him changing me over time to be more like Jesus.
- I see more and more fruit of the Spirit in my life—love, joy, peace, patience, kindness, goodness, faithfulness, gentleness, and self-control.

- I desire Him or, at least, I want to learn to desire Him more than anything else.
- Things of this world begin to be less and less important. I am willing to give up "friendship with the world" to have friendship with God.
- Things of God begin to be more and more important and interesting.
- I want to hear His voice and obey Him. I learn to recognize His voice, and I want to be quick to do whatever He commands.
- I want to spend time with Him.
- I want to please God rather than people.
- I want to hear solid Bible teaching and preaching. I have a spiritual appetite.
- I am willing to receive life-giving rebukes from God and from mature, godly, wise believers.
- I want everyone to know Jesus.
- I want to know God more and more. I desire to be in His presence.
- I am passionate about God, and I want to be even more on fire for Him.
- I have His peace and joy in my heart increasingly.
- I want to love God above everything in life and love other people with His love.
- If I see that I am putting anything above Christ in my life and heart, I am grieved and am willing to get rid of it, no matter how painful it might be.
- I am willing to be content with what I have because my contentment comes from Christ Jesus, not my circumstances.
- I am willing to learn to be thankful for suffering, knowing God is using it to prune, refine, and mature me.
- I want to praise and thank Him.
- I want to pray.
- I want to bless others.

- I want to take care of the poor, the oppressed, and those who are hurting.
- I want to love those who mistreat me and respond rightly when I am sinned against.
- I want to forgive and not hold on to bitterness.
- The Bible is alive to me—I know God is speaking to me through it, and I want to read it.
- I can't be comfortable living in sin.
- I want to humble myself before God and become less and less so that God can become more and more in my life.
- God refines my motives and points out my selfishness, pride, self-righteousness, control, idolatry, jealousy, lust, disrespect, contempt, unforgiveness, bitterness, materialism, greed, sexual immorality, and so forth, and I want to get rid of those things ASAP.
- I recognize that it is His power that is changing me, not my own. He begins to radically change my heart, mind, and soul as I invite Him to. I am willing and thankful to grant Him access to allow Him to change me.
- I want my motives to simply be that I love God and want to please Him.
- Guilt and fear no longer motivate me. Love does.

Of course, this is a process. None of us will be perfect until heaven. I grow from being a baby in Christ to being a mature adult in Him. If I belong to Jesus, He will change me and I will respond to His voice. There are times when it is harder to hear Him. Sometimes this is because of sin in my life. Sometimes I am under the enemy's attack or I am very run down—weak or exhausted or sick. Sometimes I stumble. Sometimes there are dry seasons. In general, however, the direction of my life is moving away from sin toward Jesus, and I continue to purposely seek Him far above everything and everyone else.

Resources for Studying the Bible

Desiring God is pastor John Piper's website. John Piper is also chancellor at Bethlehem College and Seminary. The site has thousands of blog posts and sermons about almost every imaginable topic relating to the Christian life. Piper authors many of the posts, but he also has other ministers and writers who help.

Go to www.desiringgod.org, and type in the search bar, "How to study the Bible."

Got Questions Ministry is a parachurch organization that is led by S. Michael Houdmann. It is one of my favorite sites to find quick answers for theological questions and real-life practical questions.

Go to www.gotquestions.org, and type in the search bar, "How to study the Bible."

Radical is the website of David Platt, a former pastor who is now the president of the International Missions Board. It provides access to his sermons, videos, and books.

Go to www.radical.net; click on "Sermons"; and then type in the search bar, "How to study the Bible."

The following are Bible sites with search capabilities to help you find verses by searching for specific words or topics.

www.bibletools.org
www.biblegateway.com
www.openbible.org
www.precept.org

Wayne Grudem is professor of theology and biblical studies at Phoenix Theological Seminary in Arizona. Podcasts from his systematic theology are available on iTunes (itunes.apple.com/us/podcast/wayne-grudems-systematic-theology/id322844869?mt=2). He approaches deep theological issues with a desire for accuracy as well as grace, compassion, love, and humility.

Appendix D

Modeling Healthy Relationships

While I'm not responsible for my children's choices, I can prepare my children for being healthy adults as I model healthy relationships in my marriage and with my children even when they are young. Thankfully, God can empower me to be the mom that He desires me to be as I seek Him wholeheartedly. This may require me to examine my own upbringing and the ideas I have brought into my marriage and parenting so I can reject any ungodly ideas and build on God's wisdom.

Let's take a moment to examine some of our beliefs about how to relate to others that we may have developed as we were growing up. As you consider the lists on the following two pages, think first about your family when you were growing up and then about your relationships with your parents and siblings now. Perhaps you may even want to make a star beside the statements that best describe how your family members relate to one another. Then you may want to go through the lists again but think about your marriage the second time. Finally, seek to evaluate your relationships with your children to see if there are any areas God may desire you to work on.

Unhealthy relationships involve wrong motives such as pride, greed, selfishness, self-righteousness, division, bitterness, jealousy, control, idolatry (of self or other people), and hatred. Healthy relationships involve godly motives such as a pure love for God and a desire to please Him, coupled with genuine unconditional love and respect for others. Healthy relationships also involve right thinking about yourself. Some of these statements aren't spoken out loud in our relationships, but they are silently understood.

Here are some hallmarks of unhealthy relationships:

- "It is not okay to talk about your negative feelings. Only positive emotions are allowed."
- "I am responsible for your decisions, obedience to God, sins, and emotions."
- "You are responsible for my decisions, obedience to God, sins, and emotions."
- "It is your job to make me happy. If I am not happy, it's your fault."
- "Conflict is unacceptable."
- "Disagreement is not allowed."
- "You may not ask me questions or confront sin in my life. I can confront you whenever I want, of course."
- "You are not safe here emotionally."
- "Your voice is not important to me."
- "I love conditionally with strings attached. If you don't perform, I won't love you."
- "You'd better put me above everything and everyone else, including God. Pleasing me had better be the most important thing in your life."
- "I will not respect any healthy boundaries you try to set with me and will be offended if you attempt to have healthy boundaries."
- "I know what is best for you 100 percent of the time."
- "I am always right, and you are wrong if you disagree with me."
- "My approval is more important than God's approval."

- "You should be afraid of my disapproval more than anything or anyone else."
- "There is no forgiveness here. I cherish bitterness and grudges against you."
- "I expect you to meet spiritual and emotional needs in my soul that really only Christ can meet. I come into this relationship as a black hole of neediness."
- "I am going to relate to you in a sinful way that is either controlling and dominating or passive and unplugged."

Here are some hallmarks and goals of healthy relationships:

- "It is okay to talk about anything and to share all your feelings about anything—even if they are negative."
- "You are responsible for your own emotions, decisions, obedience to God, and sins."
- "I am responsible for my own emotions, decisions, obedience to God, and sins."
- "If I am not happy, it is my own responsibility to take care of my emotions and to voice what I need."
- "We will work through conflict together. Conflict is inevitable. We won't always agree. But we will always love each other and work through it as a team."
- "Conflict is an opportunity for growth. You don't have to be afraid."
- "I love you unconditionally."
- "You are safe here in every way."
- "We are kind to each other."
- "We treat each other well."
- "Love and respect are abundant in both directions in our relationship."
- "You are important to me. You are precious and very valuable."
- "Your ideas, feelings, concerns, and desires are important to me."

- "Healthy boundaries are respected and encouraged."
- "We expect each of us to put God way above anyone else or anything else. Pleasing God is the most important thing in life."
- "We know we are all ultimately accountable to God for how we treat each other."
- "We are each free to respectfully confront each other about sin in our lives when necessary. We will work together as a team against sin and the enemy."
- "We trust that God knows what is best for each of us, and we each want to seek Him individually and together."
- "We approach each other with humility."
- "There is no fear in this family—only love."
- "Grace, mercy, forgiveness, and second chances are available here."
- "I have Christ on the throne of my heart, and He meets the deepest spiritual and emotional needs of my life. I come into this relationship overflowing with spiritual abundance from Jesus."

Notes

1. Charles Hummel, *The Tyranny of the Urgent*, rev. ed. (Downers Grove, IL: InterVarsity Press, 1994), 5.
2. Wayne Grudem's podcasts are available on Christian Essentials, www.christianessentialssbc.com/messages/.
3. George Mueller, *Answers to Prayer* (Chicago: Moody Press, 2010), 84–85.
4. Elisabeth Elliot, *Passion and Purity* (Grand Rapids: Revell, 1984), 163–64.
5. *Merriam-Webster*, s.v. "play the martyr," accessed December 20, 2017, https://www.merriam-webster.com/dictionary/play%20the%20martyr.
6. *Merriam-Webster*, s.v. "divisive," accessed December 20, 2017, https://www.merriam-webster.com/dictionary/divisive.
7. "What Does the Bible Say About Bitterness?" GotQuestions.org, accessed December 20, 2017, https://www.gotquestions.org/Bible-bitterness.html.
8. Jardine Malado, "'You Killed My Friend But I'm Here to Feed You'— Christian Aid Workers Fight Hate with Love by Feeding Jailed Jihadists," *Christian Times*, September 18, 2016, http://christiantimes.com/article/aid-workers-demonstrate-love-for-enemies-by-feeding-jailed-jihadists/62887.htm.

About the Author

April has two blogs, www.peacefulwife.com for married women and www.peacefulsinglegirl.com for unmarried women. Her calling is to be a Titus 2:3–5 mentor to women, teaching them to love God wholeheartedly and to allow Him to transform them to be the women He desires them to be. She focuses especially on how women can powerfully influence, love, honor, and respect their husbands and children so the gospel of Jesus is glorified. *The Peaceful Wife* averages about 30,000 views per week from all over the world, and *The Peaceful Single Girl* averages about 15,000 views per week.

In addition, April has a YouTube channel, "April Cassidy," where she has many videos about biblical womanhood that anyone is welcome to watch. She has two Facebook pages: Peaceful Wife Blog and Peaceful Single Girl. And April's husband, Greg, has a blog for husbands at www.peacefulhusband.com.

April also hosts various conferences and enjoys speaking to women's groups. You can see upcoming events and connect with her via her website.

Nothing brings April greater joy than to see God work in people's lives and to hear the stories of the miracles He has done in their lives, marriages, and families. She believes she has found "the pearl of greatest price" in Christ, and she can't wait to share this good news with everyone she can!

What happens when a woman becomes the wife God desires her to be?

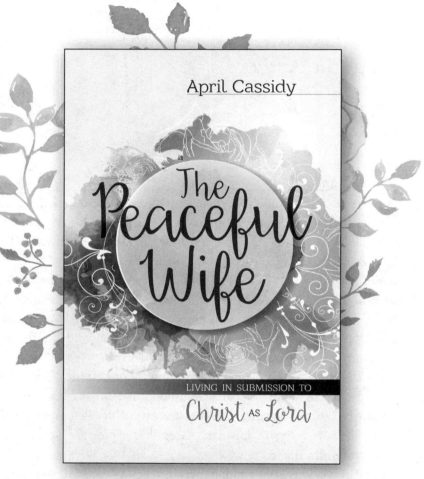

April Cassidy

The Peaceful Wife

LIVING IN SUBMISSION TO

Christ AS Lord

Learn the life-changing, joy-giving power of respect!

978-0-8254-4394-7 • $15.99